MATTHEW

MATTHEW

Go ye therefore
and teach all nations
MATTHEW 28:19

JOHN METCALFE

THE PUBLISHING TRUST
CHURCH ROAD, TYLERS GREEN, PENN, BUCKINGHAMSHIRE.

Printed and Published by
John Metcalfe Publishing Trust
Church Road, Tylers Green
Penn, Buckinghamshire

—

Distributed by Trust Representatives
and Agents world-wide

In the Far East

Bethany, Orchard Point P.O. Box 0373
Singapore 9123

—

—

First Published January 1995

—

ISBN 1 870039 61 0

—

CONTENTS

PART ONE

CHAPTERS 1 TO 13

MATTHEW

Part One

CHAPTERS 1 TO 13

IN the twenty-eight chapters of the Gospel according to Matthew, the Holy Ghost records the true nature of the Messiah—or Christ—and the real meaning of the kingdom of heaven.

This record is unfolded throughout Matthew's account of the life of Jesus in Israel, during which time the Jews' false views of the Messiah, and their erroneous concept of the kingdom, created increasing conflict, the development of which mounted from crisis to crisis until the inevitable climax in the closing chapters.

In consequence of the Jews' crucifixion of the Messiah, and their rejection of the kingdom, that kingdom was taken from them as a people and nation, and given to the Gentiles. The *ecclesia*, the church, was introduced, taking the place of Israel in the counsels of God.

Matthew refers to the word '*ecclesia*'—church—three times, the only one of the four gospels in which the word occurs. Nowhere else is there any reference to Jesus' use of this word. It is exclusive to Matthew.

The *ecclesia*, church, assembly, or congregation of Christ henceforth became the sphere in which Messiah was to administer the kingdom of God, and its present spiritual, heavenly, mysterious and divine character—resting on grace and established in sonship — unfolds prophetically and increasingly through the twenty-eight chapters of Matthew, until the full revelation is completed in the closing verses.

Matthew begins his account of the gospel with the genealogy of Messiah. It is a genealogy springing from Abraham, the father of the faithful, and heir to the promises of God. To him, and to his Seed, God promised the righteousness of faith; the resurrection from the dead; and the inheritance of the world to come.

Matthew proves by genealogy that Jesus Christ is that promised Seed, in whom all should be fulfilled. Demonstrably, he is the son of David, the son of Abraham. But if son of David, then of royal lineage.

However, if Abraham's son Isaac was raised from the dead 'in a figure', Jesus Christ was raised from the dead in truth; and if Abraham was heir to the land of Canaan in a type, Christ is heir of the world to come in reality.

Then how much more does the shadow of David's royal throne over the tribes of Israel anticipate the substance of

Christ's everlasting dominion over the sons of God, raised to life and immortality in the bliss of eternal glory, world without end?

This is the true significance of that genealogy recorded by Matthew, proving Jesus Christ to be the son of David, the son of Abraham.

But even as the carnally minded Jews denied the Messiah, confounded the genealogy, and confused the kingdom, so they missed the spiritual—and only—meaning of the shadow of the substance in David and figure of the true in Abraham. For all came to pass in Jesus Christ, whom, like their ancestors with chosen Joseph, the Jews hated without a cause.

As there is a genealogy of Jesus Christ in Matthew and in Luke but not in Mark or John, conversely there is an ascension in Mark and Luke but not in Matthew and John.

Matthew gives no account of the ascension. It is excluded by the Holy Ghost to suit the doctrine of the book. Matthew closes with Jesus, risen from the dead, meeting with the eleven on a mountain appointed in Galilee, there to admonish and command them in relation not to Israel—save for the remnant according to the election of grace—but to all nations.

Jesus had been rejected by Israel. The Jews had delivered him up to the Gentiles. The people had refused the heavenly kingdom of God, and despised with contempt the King of the Jews.

They had forsaken him, hated him, persecuted him, and denied him. Though evidently the Messiah, the son of David, the son of Abraham, him they forswore, betrayed, mocked, and condemned.

The Jews railed upon Jesus, spat upon him, passed sentence upon him, and delivered him up to be crucified. Thus they caused him to be beaten, derided, scourged, tortured and crucified. The Gentiles nailed him to and hung him upon a tree to die, as one condemned by the law, rejected by Israel, refused by the people, and accursed of God.

And as if this were not enough, three days later the Jews denied the Gentile soldiers' affirmation that he was risen from the dead, although they knew perfectly well that those soldiers had seen and heard the angel of the LORD bear witness.

The Jews refused it; they shut their minds to it; they bribed those who had seen indisputable testimony to the resurrection, persuading them to perjure themselves, to deny the sight of their own eyes, and to bear false witness for large money, being induced to lie in their teeth.

Conniving together, the Jews bribed the soldiers to put about the fable that Jesus' disciples had stolen the body, securing the troops against any future judicial enquiry by their officers.

Thus the chief priests, the assembly of the Jews, and the elders of all Israel set themselves against the work of the Father, the power of the Spirit, the resurrection of the Son, and the testimony of the angel of the LORD from the heights of heaven. They cast out their Messiah, despised the kingdom, denied the God of glory, and refused the testimony of angels.

In consequence, at the conclusion of the Gospel according to Matthew, the risen Son, the Messiah, last appears beyond the pale of Israel, looking out upon all nations from the commanding heights of the appointed mountain in Galilee of the Gentiles, there to give commandment to his disciples.

This indicates his taking a new position. Israel after the flesh, the old covenant, the legal dispensation, the earthly inheritance of the Jewish nation in this present world, are for ever rejected in the counsels of God.

Messiah is seen as risen from the dead. He is beyond that grave where all the distinctions of this life, all that belongs to this present age, everything that pertains to the world now existent, have passed away for ever.

All borders in territory; each difference of race; every diversity among flesh and blood; the vast divergence between Jew and Gentile: all nullified, voided, reduced to nothing by the dust of death and the silence of the tomb.

Christ is risen indeed. He is the other side of death, the tomb empty, time and this world forever past, with eternity and the glory of the everlasting inheritance before him.

There he is seen, poised in the new resurrection position in which all is fulfilled in himself, this Man of God's purpose, this heir of all the promises, this elect to whom pertains the world to come.

He appears as the Surety of the new testament, the Mediator of a better covenant, the King of glory, heir to an unending dominion, the everlasting Priest with eternal redemption founded on perfect sacrifice, to bring in better things to come, which should never pass away.

From this position—but only from this position—he would receive the lost sheep of the house of Israel, God's people whom he foreknew, the remnant according to the election of grace. That is, to the Jew first.

Yes, but from this position—and only from this position—he would receive the called from among the Gentiles also, from all nations, as he saith also in Osee, 'I will call them my people, which were not my people; and her beloved, which was not beloved'. For in the place where it was said, 'Ye are not my people; there shall they be called the children of the living God.'

As to Israel, he saith 'Though the number of the children of Israel be as the sand of the sea'—yet, from this evangelical position of the resurrection manifested on the mount in Galilee—'a remnant'—no more—'a remnant shall be saved.'

This is that to which the closing scene and position in Matthew allude. It is the appearance of the risen Son lingering on the mountain in Galilee of the Gentiles, above and outside of Israel, and yet with the whole land of Israel spread away to the south.

This is the position of grace in the new testament 'to the Jew first'. Grace to be preached to all Israel, yes, but from a position far above Israel, outwith the land, outside of this world, beyond time, past death, from the resurrection and the glory. And this holds good for time and eternity.

Here is a last view, whilst their rejected Messiah lingers on earth, so soon to depart. But in Matthew, where no ascension is recorded, lingering still, that all Israel might hear the witness of grace and of righteousness by faith in the evangel from distant and despised Galilee.

Wherefore? That they might forsake the old, finished, carnal, earthly, and past legal testament, and enter by Jesus Christ, the son of David, the son of Abraham, into the new, glorious, spiritual, mysterious, heavenly, evangelical and everlasting covenant.

It was already abundantly evident that, as a nation, Israel would reject the new covenant ministered from the glory by the risen Son. Nevertheless, not being of him that willeth, nor of him that runneth, but of God that showeth mercy, that the purpose of God according to election might stand, a remnant should be saved.

'What then? Israel hath not obtained that which he seeketh for; but the election hath obtained it, and the rest were blinded, according as it is written, God hath given them a spirit of slumber, eyes that they should not see, and ears that they should not hear, unto this day.'

But Esaias is very bold, saying of the Gentiles, 'I was found of them that sought me not; I was made manifest unto them that asked not after me. But to Israel he saith, All day long I have stretched forth my hands unto a disobedient and gainsaying people.' This prophecy was fulfilled when Jesus Christ, risen from the dead, heir of the world to come, commanded his disciples to go and teach all nations.

In Galilee of the Gentiles Jesus gathered to himself his eleven disciples—Mt. 28:16—to impart to them his closing commandments on earth. *Disciples* is the operative word.

Disciples: thoroughly disciplined according to all the words of this life. Nonetheless, a last solemn reminder of apostasy and death pressed upon them: *Eleven* disciples? But up to so short a time before there had been *Twelve* disciples. 'Judas, one of the twelve, which also betrayed him.'

What warnings against presumption; what urgings to constant self-denial; what necessities for daily taking up the cross, thus pressed home upon the heart of the eleven. What prayer; what supplication; what fear; what trembling; what breathings after God to be kept in lowly obedience to the Master, and meek humility with one another.

Judas, says Peter, 'Was numbered with us, and took part in this ministry.' However, Luke tells us, 'Judas by transgression fell.' For all that; for all their own weakness; for all that each one forsook Jesus and fled; for all that Peter denied him: still, eleven stood on the mount in Galilee.

By faith the eleven obeyed the voice of the Lord, gathering to him who had risen from the dead, on the mountain appointed in Galilee of the Gentiles. A place high, elevated, nearest to heaven, farthest from earth, outside of Israel: a place where there was nothing, but nothing, and no one, but no one, save Christ.

This was the place from which he commanded them, in the knowledge that all power was given unto him in heaven and in earth. Power, authority, for what? For the *eleven* to go *therefore* and *teach* all nations.

This apostolic calling admits of no others. Except the twelfth: that unique 'apostle to the Gentiles', whom the Lord was yet to call from heaven 'as one born out of due time'.

Others may be called by the Lord, and by him alone, to submit in continuance, echoing this apostolic ministry in their day and generation. But the uniqueness, the authority, the signs, belonging to *the eleven*, gave to their teaching a paramountcy to which all following ministry must of necessity be wholly subject and entirely obedient.

Jesus commands the *eleven*, whom first he had disciplined, to whom first he had imparted his doctrine, whom first he had chosen to be with him. Having been with him, they had imbibed and obeyed all that he had taught them, recorded from the first verse of the first chapter, till the last verse of the last chapter, of the Gospel according to Matthew.

These chosen vessels, and these alone, were sent in the apostolic office in and by the authority of the risen Son from the other side of death. Charged with divine, heavenly power, to bring in disciples from all nations. And to gather them *by teaching*. 'Go ye therefore, and *teach* all nations.' They were sent to *teach*. That is what the new testament is about: teaching.

But teaching what? Not teaching the literal following of Jesus' physical presence in the days of his flesh. Those days were over. Then, teaching the spiritual and interior following of all that Jesus 'began to do and to teach'. Teach *that*, but in the way of the power of his resurrection, the fellowship of his sufferings, and of conformity to his death.

Teach what? Not the outward healings, visible signs, tangible wonders of the days of his flesh, the purpose of which was to bear witness to the Christ, the Son of the living God.

Then what? Not the physical cures, the exterior miracles, the material powers, evident in Messiah's life on earth, or even vested in the apostles and first disciples under their teaching in the beginning.

Then teach what? Teach the divinity, the heavenliness, the spirituality of that doctrine of which those outward, earthly, visible, and physical healings and wonders were but signs.

The miracles of Messiah and the apostolic era were the testimony of God to the teaching of the Lord *in and of itself*. It is that *doctrine*, particularly as recorded from the first to the last chapter of Matthew, that brings in the kingdom.

But taught to whom? From the text it is evident: the disciples were to teach *all nations*. Not, as it is this day, teach *all notions!* Teach all nations. 'Teaching them to observe all things whatsoever I have commanded *you*.' This is dogmatic, absolute, authoritarian. It is outside and beyond all intellectual enquiry, rational speculation, mental judgment, or opinionated debate.

'Teaching them *to observe* all things whatsoever I have *commanded* you.' If they are disciples, they observe it; they obey it. It is commanded; it is to be done; and seen to be done. If not, such hearers are not disciples, and have no part in Christ. Not according to Matthew.

Nor is this Jewish. It has nothing to do with Israel, or the Jews. Nor does it bear any relation to the old covenant, much less the law delivered by Moses: it is 'Whatsoever *I* have commanded *you*.' In *Matthew*.

The old covenant; the legal rule; Jewish privilege, were finished for ever. Now, though 'to the Jew first', it is to *all nations* as such, and the message is that of Matthew, the evangelical command of the Lord from the other side of death, from beyond this world, from outside of time, from the glory, from out of heaven, and from everlasting to everlasting.

Moreover, those who received the disciples, and submitted in obedience to the authority of Christ vested in them, were to be baptized. Not baptized unto Moses. Nor into Jordan. But 'In the name of the Father, and of the Son, and of the Holy Ghost.' This is the divine revelation in its fulness.

This is the manner of administration in the kingdom. It is a divine administration from heaven: heavenly and spiritual. It stands in sonship: it is in the name of the Father. It unites under headship: it is in the name of the Son. It abides in the interior: it is in the name of the Spirit.

This heavenly kingdom, into which the Son brings the disciples by one Spirit, is that to which the 'called-out' disciples from all nations answer in sonship. Why? Because it is by the Spirit of sonship that the faithful are baptized in the name of the Father, and of the Son, and of the Holy Ghost.

If so, the disciples are brought experimentally into an awareness of divine Persons, just as they come into a consciousness of the distinct work of each divine Person. Moreover, the disciples are led into an intuitive sense of the relation of each divine Person to the other in that divine work.

That is what the baptism signifies, and only the 'eleven'—and those in succession called with equal divinity submissively to echo their ministry—are equipped to administer *that* baptism.

And so Jesus says: 'Go *ye* therefore, and teach all nations, baptizing them in the name of the Father, and of the Son, and of the Holy Ghost: teaching them to observe all things whatsoever I have commanded *you*: and, lo, I am with you alway, even unto the end of the world. Amen.'

'Teaching them'—*who would be made disciples*—'to observe all things whatsoever I have commanded you.' The eleven were to do that. And their spiritual successors who bear their marks—and are marked by subject submission to their apostolic authority—are to do it.

Disciples were to be made by them, and made by them through teaching 'all things whatsoever I have commanded you', in such a way that disciplined observation followed.

But what was it that he had commanded them? All things that the Son had testified, the Father had wrought, and the Spirit had witnessed, between Matthew 1:1 and Matthew 28:20.

That was what was impressed upon the heart and mind of Matthew as he recorded these words. It was the record of what Jesus had commanded them precisely, and in its entirety. The body of teaching from Matthew 1:1 to Matthew 28:20.

It was to be *taught*. Not theorized: not emotionalized: not harangued: not suggested: but taught as dogmatically as it had been delivered. Otherwise it could not be conveyed, and obedience could never follow. Nothing could substitute for teaching. Nor for its concomitant discipline.

No amount of peripheral gifts or miracles—of which Judas possessed an abundance—could substitute for that which Jesus had commanded, and commanded to be taught and disciplined by whom he would, namely, the *eleven*.

The eleven, and none other. Save that, sent from the Lord in the heavenly resurrection glory, after the twelfth, there would be those successors who would continue in obedience to all that had been delivered to the eleven disciples.

Clothed with the power, and weighty with the fruit, they would be conspicuous as walking in the way, observing the method, and manifesting the marks of those unique and chosen vessels singularly sent forth to the work at the first.

Further, the disciples were not only to *teach* all nations. They were to teach all nations the *observation* of the teaching. 'Teaching them to *observe* all things.' Those who would become disciples must be submissive to the discipline. By definition.

This is a thing virtually passed away from Christendom. Then, Christendom is by so much devoid of disciples of Christ, for the ministry of the eleven has ceased to be relevant among the sects and denominations of Christianity.

The word 'disciple' from which 'discipline' derives, demonstrates and demands *observation* of the teaching beyond a peradventure. There is a discipline in the way of the Lord. It is not optional. It is not variable. It is compulsory. It is invariable. Otherwise disciples are no more disciples.

The doctrine of the eleven disciples was experimental; it was applied; it must be *observed*. Their teaching was characterized by discipleship, a way of *life*, not a school of thought. It moved the *being*, not rested in the intellect. Discipleship entailed a way of life together, and together with those sent to teach, under their discipline, in whole-hearted submission to the Lord.

Therefore the doctrine is attended by the obedience of faith. It must be so: the nature of the kingdom is divine: it is of God. Its character is heavenly: it is of heaven. Its essence is spiritual: it is brought in by the Holy Ghost. Its method is doctrinal: they were to teach. And its authority is stated: 'He said unto the *eleven*.' That is the kingdom.

And yet, despite the forewarning of the fearful state of Israel, and the terrible example of the rejection of Messiah and the kingdom by the Jews, resulting in the kingdom being taken from them and given to the Gentiles, so that it should be taught among all nations, who takes heed?

Who takes heed? Neither Jew nor Gentile, for all the prophecies that at the end of this present age—which began with the words of Matthew 28:19 'Go ye therefore and teach all nations' —it would be worse with the Gentiles in the apostasy, than ever it was with the Jews in their falling away.

This present age will conclude with a far worse unbelief, a far worse indifference, a far worse corruption, a far worse apostasy, than that of Israel when the Jews crucified their Messiah, rejected the kingdom of heaven, denied the testimony of God, and blasphemed the Holy Ghost.

Therefore their house was left unto them desolate; the kingdom was taken from them and given to a nation bearing the fruits thereof; and the wrath came upon them to the uttermost.

And now, even at this present time, today, so near the end of the age, as it was foretold, as Jesus himself had prophesied, it is already worse with the divided denominations of Christendom than ever it had been with the rebellious Jews in their day.

As the apostasy increases apace, and the end draws nearer and nearer, the true teaching, and the obedient disciples, will be regarded as sheer hindrances to the progress of the Christian religion, disgraceful stumbling-blocks, the chief obstacles to the progress of what will have become known and accepted as evangelical Christianity in the last days.

All these things are foretold and written. With what urgency therefore does such scripture stress the need for the reiteration of this teaching? But who will teach? Who does teach?

Here appears the criterion for the recovery of what has been lost: that the Lord should take aside and for long years teach today's faithful disciples and obedient successors to 'the eleven', and even now, while there is yet time, send them to 'all nations'.

And what shall they teach, who are thus called and taught of the Lord? What shall they teach, who thus follow the doctrine and observations of the eleven, called in their generation? No more and no less than that which was taught by the apostolate at the beginning. In a word, they shall teach, firstly:

The Advent of Messiah and the Kingdom, Matthew Chapters 1 to 4

These chapters form the first clear division of Matthew, and begin with the generation of Jesus Christ, the son of David, the son of Abraham, from the book of the ancestral records of the chosen seed and the royal inheritance. Jesus is indisputably both the Royal Messiah from David and the Elect Seed of Abraham by ancient prophecy.

The birth of Jesus Christ follows. He was born of the virgin Mary, who had been found with child of the Holy Ghost. Of this the angel of the Lord testified to Joseph, saying, 'That which is conceived in her is of the Holy Ghost. And she shall bring forth a son, and thou shalt call his name JESUS: for he shall save his people from their sins.'

The second chapter bears testimony to the birth of the Messiah. According to the age-old prophecy of Balaam in the days of Moses, 'There shall come a Star out of Jacob, and a Sceptre shall rise out of Israel', Numbers 24:17.

For this, far off to the east, the wise had looked from generation to generation. In the most distant parts, some two years before, that star had appeared, unique and conspicuous in the heavens.

And for two years the wise men had journeyed, following the star that signified the birth of the Saviour, the Messiah. Of this great heavenly sign, the Jews were oblivious.

To it, the Gentiles paid heed. The star, which they had seen in the east, went before them, till it came and stood over the place where the young child was. And they fell down, and worshipped him.

There follows the malice of Herod, the flight into Egypt, and the eventual return to Nazareth.

Chapter three gives the record of heaven and earth to the person of Christ. The genealogy had borne witness. The angel had borne witness. The birth had borne witness. John had borne witness. And now the opened heavens testified. The voice of the Father testified. The Holy Ghost testified.

Here is a fourfold witness and a threefold testimony beyond all dispute: 'This is my beloved Son, in whom I am well pleased.' This, the eleven were to teach, to cause disciples to observe, and those called in their turn were to continue in this doctrine even to the end of the age.

Following this, Matthew records the beginning of Jesus' ministry. The beginning of his ministry was temptation, and this from being led up of the Spirit into the wilderness, there to fast forty days and nights, following which the tempter came to him, which is called diabolos, and Satan.

But Jesus in his impeccable humanity steadfastly resisted him, dismissing him at the last with peerless superiority, and the angels came and ministered unto him.

Jesus then began to minister in Galilee, after John had been cast into prison. Jesus called certain brethren. They followed him. Disciples do follow him. They do not sit and debate, continuing the discussion after he has passed by.

'Straightway they left their nets and followed him.' 'And immediately they left the ship and their father, and followed him.' That is to be a disciple, and brethren are those who observe the discipline.

Jesus' ministry was manifested in preaching the gospel of the kingdom, healing all manner of sicknesses, diseases and torments, delivering those that were possessed with devils, the lunatic, and the palsied. He healed them all, his fame spreading from Galilee of the Gentiles to all quarters.

This concludes the first part of the evangel.

The next part follows:

The Doctrine of Messiah and the Kingdom, Chapters 5 to 7

This entire passage encompasses what is known as 'The Sermon on the Mount'. Salient features to note are the setting on the mountain; Jesus' posture; and the description of his hearers: 'Disciples' who 'came to him'.

His doctrine commenced with the description of the spiritual entrance into the kingdom of heaven, generally referred to as 'The Beatitudes'. There follows in this exposition of the gospel of the kingdom of heaven, in order, Messiah's teaching on Righteousness and the kingdom; next, Godliness and the kingdom; and, finally, Judgment and the kingdom.

The whole of this constitutes the doctrine which Jesus commanded his disciples to teach all nations, 'teaching them to observe all things whatsoever I have commanded you'.

This tremendous passage lies at the heart of the gospel, and, together with the previous section of Matthew, may be found more fully expounded in order in the book 'The Messiah', together with the excerpt separately entitled 'The Beatitudes'.*

This in its entirety is the doctrine which Jesus, the son of David, the son of Abraham, the Messiah, who was conceived of the Holy Ghost, and born of the virgin Mary, commanded to be taught and observed of all who seek the kingdom of heaven.

I would here stress the unmitigated evil of the dispensational system. Revived among the Plymouth Brethren and iniquitously inserted in the wretched 'Schofield' bible, Dispensationalism incorporates a heresy which cuts out the whole of Matthew chapters 5 to 7 as if it had no reference to the gospel, the Christian, or the church.

In this heresy it is as if Jesus' teaching in Matthew chapters 5 to 7 does not constitute a vital part of the doctrine of Christ. To the dispensationalist this central passage applies only to the Jews, and at that, in some future mythical millennium.

Whosoever believes and teaches this heinous error has denied the faith; despised the Messiah; defied the apostles; opposed the Spirit; rent the gospel asunder; contradicted Almighty God, and, in consequence, forsaken his own mercies.

*See 'The Messiah', 'Apostolic Foundation of the Christian Church' Series Volume Three, by John Metcalfe; and 'The Beatitudes', by John Metcalfe; available from The Publishing Trust. See advertising pages.

Those who do this—whosoever they be—can expect to be heard crying out 'Lord, Lord', in the judgment. But since they do not the things which he says, how can they expect any answer save 'Depart from me, I never knew you'?

Had they known him, they would have heard, observed, and kept his word, and then he would have made his abode with them. But since they relegate the whole of this doctrine to the Jews, viciously rending it out of the gospel, they can expect to receive from the Messiah the same things which they have done to him.

We ought therefore to take the more earnest heed to the things which we have heard—particularly from the Lord Jesus himself—lest at any time we should let them slip. We are to take heed whom we hear; what we hear; and how we hear.

These are the words—all the words—which at the first began to be spoken by the Lord, and were afterwards confirmed unto us by them that heard him. We are to be wise builders. We are to recall the words of Messiah that we should beware of those false prophets who come to us in sheep's clothing.

The more particularly then ought we to watch against these dispensationalists — so-called — who are no better than the wicked king who cut the scriptures with a penknife, consigning the fragments to the fire. These are they who cut out the words which at the first began to be spoken by the Lord.

'To the law and to the testimony; if they speak not according to this word, it is because there is no light in them.'

Light, however, shines from the ascended Lord in the heavenly glory through the eleven, the Spirit of truth bringing to their memory all that he had taught them, so that they went to all nations 'teaching *them* to observe *all things whatsoever* I have *commanded you*'.

This that they were to teach, which he had first taught them, of absolute necessity includes Matthew chapters 5 to 7, the very heart of the doctrine of Christ, falling from his own lips.

The third definitive passage in the Gospel according to Matthew—defined because each incident and every discourse displays a distinctive common denominator—now follows:

The Power of Messiah and the Kingdom, Chapters 8 to 9

Unclean lepers, outcast Gentiles, palsied servants, feverish women, and infirm multitudes, evidence that the power of Messiah is more than equal to the performance of his word.

But certain would-be followers must learn that the kingdom may be illustrated by but it does not stand in exterior miracles or even outward following. It stands in righteousness, peace, and joy in the Holy Ghost.

Messiah's power for the kingdom of heaven not only soars with sublime authority over all sicknesses, diseases, and legions of demons, but it is also superior to the forces which move both wind and sea, so that even the powers of heaven yield at no more than a word from the lips of Jesus.

Notwithstanding, it remains true that the kingdom of heaven does not rest even in such divine manifestations as these.

Not in the emptying and cleansing of the house, but in the divine, spiritual, mysterious and heavenly abiding within its habitation. This constitutes the house of God, the temple of the Holy Ghost, the body of Christ, the *ecclesia*, and, in a word, is the witness of the kingdom of heaven come unto you.

By the word of Messiah, in the witness to the kingdom, the paralytic is raised. But so is the enmity, malice, and ungovernable fury of the religious leaders. This, borne of bitter envy, centred in the scribes, Pharisees, priests, and rulers of the people.

The kingdom is received, yes, but this appears in the poor and needy, the publicans and sinners, the outcasts and those that are without help in any wise.

The dead are raised to life again; divers miracles follow; and what? The opposition of the chief priests, elders, scribes, Pharisees, Sadducees, doctors, lawyers, and leaders of Israel becomes more and more open, more and more blasphemous, more and more violent, with the mounting demand that Jesus should be silenced, and cut off out of the land of the living.

Much ministry follows: but the labourers are few, and if so, prayer is to be made to the Lord of the harvest to send forth labourers—*fellow*labourers—into that harvest.

Now a new, fourth, phase is reached in the narrative. Again, this is detected by the appearance of a new common denominator, distinct from that which preceded, and yet different from the tenor of all that follows thereafter. This new emphasis now unfolds in sequence:

The Rejection of Messiah and the Kingdom, Chapters 10 to 12

The twelve disciples are called unto Jesus, and given power against unclean spirits, to cast them out, and to heal all manner of sickness, and all manner of disease. The names of the twelve apostles are recorded.

These twelve Jesus sent forth into all Israel, avoiding the way of the Gentiles and every city of the Samaritans. As they went, they were to preach, saying, The kingdom of heaven is at hand. They were to heal the sick, cleanse the lepers, raise the dead, and cast out demons. These were the unique signs of an apostle, and this was their unique testimony to Israel.

After this, the scope of Jesus' commandment widens prophetically to embrace the days when the apostles should be sent to the Gentiles of all nations.

The consequent rejection of the apostles by those nations is foretold.

The apostles will be delivered up to councils, scourged in synagogues, brought before governors and kings for Messiah's sake, for a testimony against them, and the Gentiles.

Therefore those who are sent, and the disciples made by them, find themselves in the midst of a world full of enmity, a world rejecting the testimony which the apostles are to hold fast under torture and unto death, in the fear of God.

Disciples are to confess Christ, accepting the gospel sword of separation, even though it cuts to the dividing asunder of their own families. They are to honour and take up the cross, lose their life to find it, and suffer on earth among men the shame and reproach of Christ and of the gospel of the kingdom of heaven above everything else.

And whosoever receives those whom Christ sends, God shall honour commensurately, beyond this present rejecting world, in the eternal ages of the glory yet to come.

The apostles departed to travel throughout all Israel. Then Jesus himself departed likewise, following in their steps who went before to prepare the way, preaching and teaching throughout all their cities. This twofold testimony demanded a response from Israel to Messiah and the kingdom.

The issue had been raised with a witness: Now that issue must be answered, and the response given. For 'Jesus made an end of teaching'. Yes, but with what effect, all Israel having received first the witness of the apostles, and then the testimony of Jesus himself?

John the Baptist had run his course; next the apostles had completed their mission; finally, Jesus himself had followed and duly 'made an end of teaching'.

This ministry of Christ was attested not only by his own wondrous works, but those of his Father in heaven, accompanied by the witness of the Spirit on earth, the whole fulfilling the scriptures of the prophets, the very oracles of God.

It was no longer a question of further light. It was a question of how Israel had responded to the full light that had been made manifest in all their coasts. What was the response to the light of that glory of the Messiah which had been testified, and which had shone, throughout their land?

The rulers and the nation of Israel totally rejected the light both of Messiah and the kingdom. And why? Because they loved darkness rather than light.

This appears throughout the crucial passage in Matthew chapter 11. This is the turning point in the counsel of God toward Israel as a nation. A climax has been reached. At this point testimony has been rendered to the utmost both as to the person and work of Messiah, and the heavenly and spiritual nature of the kingdom.

Already the response of controlled envy and suppressed malice had made itself known. But now, after full apostolic and Messianic witness, all comes to light. Israel's response was drawn out and fully exposed: rejection was total, outright, and irrevocable. This was the criterion.

At this point Jesus exposes the moral disaster of the rejection of Messiah and the kingdom on the part of the Jewish nation, by comparative examples.

He points to those cities where his mighty works were done, Chorazin and Bethsaida—for instance—and compares them with the Gentile cities of Tyre and Sidon. They received no Messianic visits, had no apostles sent unto them, saw no mighty works, and heard nothing of the coming kingdom of heaven.

Yet had these Gentile cities been given the same testimony as that of the despising and rejecting Jewish cities of Chorazin and Bethsaida, they would have repented long ago in sackcloth and ashes!

Woe, Woe, therefore, to the Jewish despisers: it would be worse for them in the day of judgment, than for Tyre and Sidon. And, yes, even *Sodom*—of all places—would fare better in the day of judgment than Capernaum: 'for if the mighty works done in Capernaum had been done in Sodom, it would have remained unto this day.'

Then had the despising of Messiah, and the rejection of the kingdom, brought so ancient and extended a work of God throughout the old testament to nothing, because of the froward and wicked enmity of that generation of the Jews in Israel? God forbid.

By no means. God and the Father foresaw all, and now by Jesus Christ brings to light the mystery hidden from ages and from generations, the divine purpose kept secret from the foundation of the world. At this climactic point appears the first disclosure, the dawning beams of the revelation of the mystery.

Despite the worst and most incorrigible enmity against God by the most religious of men; despite that this was manifested under the greatest light ever to shine in the world; God's grace had an answer to man's depravity. Henceforth God would choose the poor, the foolish, the weak, the despised, and the things which are not, to bring to nought the things that are. The Father would beget a people to himself by the interior revelation from heaven of the glory of the Son. Moreover the Son would reveal the Father.

Here appears a mystery of divinity outside and beyond all human capacity and capability, past all that eye could see, or ear could hear, or the mind of man could comprehend.

Passing every dimension comprehensible to man, this was a mystery standing in the revelation of the deity, and determined within the deity: the revelation of the Father and of the Son.

'No man knoweth the Son but the Father, and neither knoweth any man the Father, save the Son, and he to whomsoever the Son will reveal him.'

After all the record of John; all the testimony of the apostles; all the mighty works of the Messiah; all the power of the kingdom; all the attestation of the Father; all the witness of the Spirit, and all the fulfilment of the scriptures: No man, no, not one single man, comprehended the mystery of Christ.

Thus these things—these divine mysteries of the kingdom —were hid from the wise and prudent. That was the judgment of God. But the same mysteries were revealed unto babes. That was the election of God. You see that it is revelation and mystery. The babes did not do it: the Father did it to them.

Of such would be—and is—the kingdom of heaven, and that by the revelation of the mystery. This stood alone in the Father's prerogative.

This revelation came to light in consequence of the total and irremediable rejection of Messiah and the kingdom by man in his greatest darkness: that is, when most religious. Nevertheless, God would bring in the hidden mystery.

The Son would be made known by interior revelation from the Father in heaven. And in the light of that heavenly glory the Son would reveal the Father. Thus the kingdom would prosper in his hand world without end.

What Israel had rejected, the Father would raise up in the *ecclesia*, the congregation of the living God, the pillar and ground of the truth. He would preserve and magnify his own work in the 'babes' begotten from on high.

With this revelation following Israel's manifest blindness and malice, next the Jews ascribe to the prince of the demons, Satan, the very things of Messiah and the kingdom. Now they are determined to destroy him. The narrative hastens on apace:

The Prophecy of Messiah and the Kingdom, Chapter 13

Here Jesus teaches seven prophetic and largely parallel parables concerning the consequence and future of the kingdom of heaven. These prophesy of greater profession than possession even at the very beginning. They speak of subsequent successive generations becoming more and more corrupt till at the last virtually the whole becomes rotten.

Only at the resurrection from the dead with the manifestation of the wheat and the tares, the sheep and the goats, will it become clear what was and what was not of the kingdom. So that not until the day of judgment would all that is of God be gathered to glory out of all the generations which preceded, from first to last.

These parallel parables are not to give direction to the saints in the midst of increasing decay. Much less are they to provide an excuse for not taking that pathway of separation so clearly taught elsewhere.

These seven parables foretell the inception, infiltration, and permeation of corruption, hardly visible in the beginning but overwhelming at the end. The parables give the history of the sowing and effect of the word of the kingdom throughout time till the day of judgment. Nothing else.

History will repeat itself. The course of the prophecy follows the path of history. As it was at the first with the seed of Abraham, the father of the faithful, so it will be at the last with the seed of the kingdom sown by Messiah.

For the spiritual seed of Abraham was originally parallel with but was soon overtaken by a vastly greater and more prolific carnal number, alike owning the same progenitor.

These numerically superior bondchildren claimed Abraham to their father, but they were neither partakers of his grace nor followers of his faith. In the end they took over all Israel. So it would be in the kingdom. The 'babes' in whose good ground the seed was sown, would be overwhelmed in number by the hardened, superficial, and worldly majority.

Such carnal and empty would-be disciples—called wayside, shallow, and thorny ground hearers—would increase until, numerically superior, they would swamp and usurp the kingdom—the 'church'—just as completely as had their counterparts swamped and usurped the spiritual seed of Abraham in the history of Israel.

The coming in of the multitude of these usurpers—at first indistinguishable in the common reception of the same seed —would wax worse and worse, till the kingdom at the end of this present age would bear no resemblance at all to its appearance in the beginning.

Judgment, terrible and inexorable, fiery and overwhelming, immutable and everlasting, will appear in the coming day of retribution.

This will result in an eternal separation of the true from the false—the sheep from the goats—alike raised from the dead out of all generations, reaching even to that selfsame hour in which Jesus spoke these prophetic parables as he sat in the ship addressing the multitudes on the sea-shore in Galilee.

That concluding day will confirm the commencing prophecy: to divide to heaven and to hell; to bliss and to anguish; to the everlasting inheritance of the blessed of the Father, and to the weeping, wailing, and gnashing of teeth of the cursed of God in the unquenchable furnace of fire.

So prophesied the Messiah of the effect, consequence, progress and conclusion of the sowing of the seed of the gospel of the kingdom.

PART TWO

CHAPTERS 14 TO 28

Part Two

CHAPTERS 14 TO 28

The Revelation of Messiah and the Kingdom, Matthew Chapters 14 to 18

THIS title is no arbitrary heading, any more than are those which divide the first thirteen chapters of Matthew, noticed in the preceding exposition. There is a sharp distinction between each section, easily detected by observing the common denominator peculiar to the signs, miracles, or discourses which constitute that part of the gospel.

This common denominator creates a character unique to each particular division. The observation of this sets apart any one section from that which preceded and everything which follows. This will appear in the opening now before us, namely, The Revelation of Messiah and the Kingdom, Chapters 14 to 18.

All the incidents in Chapters 14 to 18 have in common that which binds them together, so that taken as a whole, and seen in relation to the previous teaching of Matthew up to Chapter 14, the sixth division presents its own distinctive message, unique to these five chapters of the book.

Here is a division of tremendous importance in the revelation of the mystery of the gospel. The passage begins with the death of John, and it ends with the disappearance of Moses and Elijah.

This tells us that the coming spiritual and heavenly kingdom has nothing to do with the law; with works; with an earthly temple; with a carnal priesthood; sacrificial ministry; or the observance of sabbaths; new moons; or days; or any other thing that stood in Israel under the old covenant.

It is a new thing: another thing: it is a revelation. It is entirely to do with the heavenly mystery; with the revelation of that mystery; divinely brought in and inwardly wrought by Father, Son, and Holy Ghost.

Chapter 14 shows that the time under the law of the old covenant had run its course, ending with the rejection of Messiah and the kingdom. Nevertheless, a remnant of Israel according to the election of grace would be divinely fed with heavenly bread by their Messiah in the coming new testament. These shall never perish.

There can never be any return to the old, failed, legal rule. The heart of man—Chapter 15—is the root of defilement, and makes unclean from within all that man would do for God under the law; 'All our righteousnesses are as filthy rags.' The inward parts of man are both defiled and incorrigible.

The law had shown that; and shown that it was incapable of rectifying it: rather, the law made the condition worse. It awakened sin, excited its motions, stirred up its rebellion, and generated its enmity; just as it brought down a heavy yoke, an unbearable burden, a dreadful curse, and a sentence of death.

From this fearful condition, that is, the condition of man brought to light under the rigours and obligations of the law, nothing save Messiah and the kingdom could bring deliverance and give hope.

It is this deliverance and hope that appears in the true bread from heaven given by the Father, personified by the Son, and inwrought by the Holy Ghost, being administered through the apostles to the poor remnant, depicted in the feeding of the five thousand.

For the rest, the wrath has come upon them to the uttermost, because the old covenant had brought to light the bitter enmity of heart against God, in all those who sought righteousness by the works of the law.

Then nothing will suffice save a new creation. No less, indeed, than a new man in Christ: a new heart, a new spirit, the old having been judged, condemned, and put away.

This new beginning commences in the inward parts, in the hidden man of the heart. It springs from union with him who walked upon the water, in whom the law of the Spirit of life rises over all that sinks beneath the law of sin and death. The one buoys up over every law given below; the other submerges beneath every wave of sin, plunging under the waters of death. Life, however, is ascendant.

It is just this that Messiah came to bring in, and just here that the kingdom of heaven begins its rule and dominion. Following on from the divine feeding of the Jewish remnant, Christ now feeds the starving Gentile multitude also, in a figure giving succour to the famished through righteousness unto eternal life by heavenly manna in the inner man.

This makes of twain, Jew and Gentile, one new man in Christ, so breaking down the middle wall of partition between both. Here is depicted that new creation, with the spiritual man, sustained by heavenly food, inwardly and divinely nourished by Messiah.

The number fed, first five thousand then four thousand, signifies those called out and separated first from the remnant of Israel and then from the poor Gentiles of all nations.

This world is depicted as a wilderness unable to feed the hunger of the spiritual. Those redeemed from out of the world appear in the sign of the prophet Jonas, with life in and from Christ, who died for their sins, and was raised from the dead on their behalf by the glory of the Father.

For, Chapter 16, the Jews in their self-righteous, self-justifying, legal religion are blind and dead both to the Messiah and to the kingdom: and if this be so of divinely chosen and shepherded Israel, how much more of the benighted Gentiles?

It is an evil generation out of Adam in the Fall, corrupt at the heart, and, as to any movement to Godward, rotten to the core, dead to all that is heavenly and spiritual.

From whence it follows that any work suited to the divine nature must be all of God, and it must be all of grace. For with man, cultivated generation by generation in Israel over the centuries, and above all this, at the point of the brightest revelation of the love of God, and presence of Christ, What appears? Nothing but blindness and thick darkness.

Not a glimmer, not the least ray, appears. Incorrigible, ineradicable, unalterable total depravity of heart prevent a single beam of light from the presence of their Messiah, and the imminence of the kingdom, either opening the eyes of the Jews, or penetrating their darkness.

Indeed, the light of Messiah and the kingdom show up that moral blindness and blackness to the depths of its enmity against all that is divine, all that is heavenly, and all that is spiritual.

When asked whom men said that he was, the confusion and sightlessness of Israel was total. Some said one thing, some another; but not one knew him for whom he was, and not one failed to be enraged when testimony was rendered to his true identity.

However his own disciples knew, because they had been given sight and enlightenment from within by the heavenly revelation of the Son from the Father. And that was the divine answer to human rejection.

God had before time predestined his response, his answer, to the rejection of the Messiah and the kingdom of heaven by Israel. That answer lay in his own Son: it was in Christ. It is called '*the ecclesia*', the 'church'. But it is *his* church. And *he* is its Builder.

Here for the first time the word 'church' falls from the lips of Jesus, Matthew 16:18, in the only gospel—*the kingdom gospel*—where *ecclesia*, or 'church' occurs. 'My church': how different from that which is of *men*. '*Our* church.' Christ's *ecclesia* is built by himself, in person: 'I will build.' Christ's *ecclesia* is built on rock: '*On this rock* I will build.'

This is the rock of the revelation of the Son from the Father in heaven. 'Flesh and blood hath not revealed it unto thee, but my Father which is in heaven.'

On *this* rock, the rock of revelation, interior and spiritual, heavenly and divine, indwelling and mysterious, from the Father's inward illumination of the Son, the Messiah builds his *ecclesia*, or church, by uniting or building together those whom he perceives have received this same revelation.

Nothing else warrants the term 'church'. It is exclusive to this rock, just as it is unique to Messiah's building.

This further revelation expounds exactly what was made manifest after the rejection of Messiah and the kingdom, recorded in the climax of Matthew 11:25 to 27. This is that rock, in which the Father reveals the Son to babes, and likewise hides everything from the wise and prudent.

This is that same—and only—rock of revelation to those in whom the Father in heaven chooses to reveal his Son by the Holy Ghost: and to whom, in turn, the Son inwardly reveals the Father by the same Spirit. Of these, Christ builds his church. There is no other building but this one building.

In such 'babes' the Father reveals the Son by the light of the heavenly glory breaking within the inner man; all who receive this revelation are one: called out, to be built—on this rock—so as to form the *ecclesia*, or 'church'. To those subject to this divine work of the Father and the Son, the proper use of the word 'church' is peculiar.

There are keys to this. The keys are the teaching, or doctrine, given to the apostles: *the doctrine of Messiah and the kingdom.* Nothing else, and no one else, unlocks the door. No other keys fit. There are no other keyholders.

The apostolic doctrine of the gospel fits: *provided it is in the mouth of the apostles, or those chosen in turn submissively to promulgate their doctrine.* That is what the Father, the Son, and the Holy Ghost use to grant admission into the revelation of the mystery, and these are the chosen vessels used to turn the keys in that divine administration.

Hence, as to the doctrine: 'Go ye therefore and teach all nations'. And, as to the turning of the keys, 'baptizing them in the name of the Father, and of the Son, and of the Holy Ghost'; finally, as to admission, 'teaching them to observe all things whatsoever I have commanded you.'

And if any enquire as to succession of administration: 'Lo, I am with *you*'—*you*, mark it, and none other—'with *you* always, *even unto the end of the world.*' That period exceeding the lifetime of the eleven, a principle of succession inevitably follows. With these words, the gospel according to Matthew closes.

In Chapter 17 Christ is transfigured: but not anywhere; not to anyone; nor at any time. The wise will note the day, the place, and the persons to whom the vision was manifested, besides the visionary appearance of Moses and Elias, alike their disappearance, and, above all, the testimony of the Father from heaven. Nor will they miss the effect of the vision: 'They fell on their face, and were sore afraid.'

Without such revealed transfiguration, and its effects, there can be no impact, neither vision, nor could there follow the essential divine consequences. Then, there could be no church. For without the heavenly vision, there is nothing but hypocritical pretence. But with it, the effect is inevitable: 'They fell on their face, and were sore afraid.'

Hence it is written, 'Fear came upon every soul', Acts 2:43. Once more, 'Great fear came upon all the church', Acts 5:11. Thus, and only thus, 'They saw no man, save Jesus only', Matthew 17:8. Moses and Elias had disappeared from view.

But these are disciples, perhaps the most common word used to describe those brought to faith. Disciples are babes who have lost their lives, not saved them. Who took up their daily cross, not dropped it. Who gained their souls, not lost them. And who kept the last Judgment, and the resurrection, and being judged according to works, in their heart, and in their vision, to the very end. Amen.

These babes are God's answer to a carnal, scripture-quoting, Christ-hating, religion-professing Israel after the flesh, and, in turn, to a Gentile apostasy, increasingly rebellious against these selfsame spiritual verities, till such truths have wellnigh passed from either memory or recognition. Fools and blind! 'For the word of the Lord endureth for ever.'

In Chapter 17, following the vision of the glory of the risen Son, there is that which has waxed old, and is ready to pass away. Christ is all. His doctrine—from his own lips—is everything. His death is our deliverance, his resurrection our life, his inheritance our glory. Sonship appears uniquely in this and the next chapter.

The nature and value of the unity of 'little ones'—separated from an offending world and surrounded by an offended religion—remains inestimable in the sight of God and the Father. There is the question of offensive brethren also: these are the cause of strife and disunity.

Here again Jesus speaks the word '*ecclesia*' or 'church'. After the first use of this word in Mt. 16:18, there is a twofold repetition in Mt. 18:17. This is the final occurrence of the word '*ecclesia*' in any of the gospels: the references are unique to Matthew, who records the only occasions on which this word was spoken by Jesus himself. In the '*ecclesia*', or 'church', the value of unity abides inestimable.

Resource is given to brethren in unity, to maintain their unbroken oneness in the face of those who offend in the *ecclesia*. The character of brethren is described. It is character that will and must mark all those admitted by Messiah into the kingdom till the end of the world.

The seventh division of Matthew follows:

The Testimony of Messiah and the Kingdom, Chapters 19 to 25

In Chapters 19 to 20 Jesus teaches in Judea beyond Jordan, as, slowly, he makes his way with his disciples to Jerusalem.

He heals multitudes. He silences the Pharisees who came to him with deceitful questions, the answers to which were irrelevant to them, whose single purpose was to trap him in his words. But they are trapped in their own words.

Jesus speaks of marriage, little children, and eternal life. He contrasts eternal life with all that was given by Moses, the law, the old covenant, and the earthly land of inheritance in Israel. He teaches of riches, of forsaking all, and of the glory consequent upon following him. He delivers the parable of the labourers in the vineyard.

He prophesies to the twelve of his betrayal at Jerusalem to the chief priests and scribes, and of their delivering him to the Gentiles to mock, scourge, and crucify; and the third day he shall rise from the dead.

As if he had said nothing, immediately the mother of Zebedee's children, with her sons, begs the chief place in the kingdom. This caused dissension among the ten. Jesus teaches them to take the lowest place, not connive for the highest.

Departing from Jericho, he pities two blind men, whom others would have silenced. Jesus stands still, hearing the anguished cry of the blind, desperate in their last and only hope of ever being able to see. He came and touched their eyes, granting them sight in his compassion. They follow him.

Chapters 21 and 22 report what for doctrinal purposes in Matthew appears to be Jesus' first entry into Jerusalem followed by his visit to the temple. Out of three successive entries at this period, Matthew records only two. In Matthew it is as if Jesus had never been to Jerusalem before. Here it is 'Thy King cometh unto thee!'

We are to learn the lesson that doctrine, and the deliberate omission or inclusion of events to suit the doctrine, govern the narrative: not chronological order.

What godless rubbish the so-called theological and divinity schools and lecturers teach: as if the gospels were four amateur scrap-books of faded memory, lost sources, and disparate random, written by careless bunglers so inept that they lacked the *nous* to compare what they were about to write with what their contemporaries had already written! And to crown all this, apparently the three synoptic evangelists first forgot to mention then lost all record of that priceless 'Q' on which they were supposed to be so dependent. Very likely.

However, turning from the counsel of the ungodly, abhorring the stance of sinners, and fleeing the seat of the scorner, we attend rather to the words which the Holy Ghost teacheth, and the order of them, in each separate gospel, presenting breath-taking doctrine and divinity, spiritual beyond comparison, marshalled to divine perfection, harmonized with superlative balance, and presented with unique heavenliness.

On this first—in Matthew—entry into Jerusalem, Jesus goes up in majesty to the temple. His authority is undeniable. He heals the blind and the lame; he condemns the money-making apostasy; he receives the praise of babes and sucklings; and he earns the undying enmity of the hypocritical priests and scribes.

He leaves them, the temple, and their city, as, put to silence, they gnash their teeth in impotent rage. They fume, yes, whilst ignoring the fact that for the first time their temple had been hallowed. This was their shame. They counted as nothing the miracles wrought before their eyes that day, miracles not seen since the foundation of the world. Thus far, the first entry in Matthew.

The last entry follows. The incident of Jesus cursing the barren fig tree, that it should bear no fruit henceforth for ever, and its presently withering away, occurs on the journey from Bethany to the city. This signifies the perpetual curse upon the fruitless and barren nation of Israel and the Jews.

Nothing in current events—or post-war history—concerning those called Jews today, returning to that called Israel, or to Jerusalem below, alters Jesus' word, or changes his 'for ever'. Premillennialism remains the gospel-destroying heresy the father of lies made it from the beginning. Let the unstable be blown about, or become excitable, as they will: it is all light as air.

Christ; the kingdom; the gospel: here is the rock. Here is the only stability. Here alone are the things secure for eternity. As to the Jewish nation, the land, the legal system, Jesus' curse rests on it: 'Henceforth for ever.'

Individual Jews who would be saved must renounce all, believing the same, the only, the everlasting gospel preached for salvation without a difference to Jew and Gentile alike.

Henceforth, men shall pass by and hiss from generation to generation, saying, 'This is the nation that rejected Messiah and the kingdom of heaven brought nigh unto them.' The disciples are encouraged in this very incident to believe without doubting, and their faith shall not only wither fig trees, but cast mountains into the sea.

And when he was come into the temple, the chief priests and elders of the people came to him, burning with rage from the previous day when they had been obliged impotently to watch as the glory of Christ was manifested in his own temple, the majesty of the King was hailed in his own city, and the miracles of the Son bore testimony from his own Father.

Having gathered their strength, now they will challenge his authority, oblivious to the fact that they, and the people and nation ruled by them, had been depicted by the fig tree about whose cursing they knew nothing. Speaking of the things which he had done on the previous day, they say, 'By what authority doest thou these things? And who gave thee this authority?'

These things? What! 'The wonderful things which he did', Mt. 21:15? What! 'Healing *the blind* and curing *the lame*', Mt. 21:14? What authority could possibly invest and fulfil such things, but that of Almighty God?

Who gave him this authority? None other than Almighty God, who had not given them anything, least of all their trumped-up, dressed-up, mocked-up pretence, together with their thought-up honours, got-up titles, and heaped-up flatteries which they bestowed one upon another. But there was the rub: Almighty God had surely sent and blessed Messiah, but he had certainly neither sent nor blessed them.

They sent and blessed each other. And this is the cause of persecution even to the present day. As the spirit that was in them envied and raged against the Spirit that was in Jesus, so the like spirit in our persecutors envies and rages against the same Spirit of Christ that is in us to this very hour.

But he condescends to answer them. Or, rather, question them. They dare not answer. They make fools of themselves before all the people. 'We cannot tell', they grudgingly mutter. But they could tell. And so could all the people. And yet those very people would soon be turned round by these same leaders, mindlessly to rage, beyond all reason, 'Crucify him! Crucify him!'

Jesus' parables of the two sons of the vineyard owner; of the absent husbandman and the tenants of his vineyard; and of the marriage feast of the king's son: all convince the Jews to their teeth. The Pharisees take counsel to entangle him in his talk, but, over Caesar's penny, they are entangled in their own talk.

Next come the Sadducees, sniggering with levity among themselves at what they suppose to be their eminent wit, but slinking away in shame at the exposure of their vain and empty lightness. A lawyer tempts Christ. But the solemn and weighty words of the Messiah leave him speechless, convinced in his judgment but untouched in his enmity.

Last, Jesus asks them one question. They are utterly dumbfounded. It was not merely that they were unable to answer. It was more that they had never so much as thought of such a question. What? And these lead the people? If so, then the blind lead the blind.

Finally, Chapter 23, religious sects and their leaders, personified by the scribes and Pharisees, hypocrites—that is, every possible development of the flesh in the things of God—are perfectly condemned by Jesus with a sevenfold woe.

They are stripped of pretence and deceit, being denounced as proud, divisive, and destructive hypocrites who have stolen the things of God, assumed places to which they were never called, and acted parts to which they had no title, bringing to ruin the testimony of Israel. Jesus' words are perfectly scathing; totally exposing; and completely condemning.

Israel as a nation is cast out, Jerusalem with its temple is to be destroyed, and her house is to be left unto her desolate. Whilst these words are wrung from Messiah with indignation and wrath for all that had been lost, for all who had been slain, it was not without moving pathos that Jesus pronounced such a judgment.

None but Messiah knew the finality of the judgment that must be brought to pass. But just as Jesus knew with prophetic certainty, so the people were blinded by unbelieving perversity concerning that inevitable judgment which the Jews had brought upon themselves by their haughty presumption and obdurate hardness.

In the final chapter of this section Jesus reveals the apocalyptic vision of the end of the temple, of Jerusalem, and of the world. This apocalypse is woven together with Jesus' prophecy of the enlargement of the kingdom, that is, of the *ecclesia*, soon to become greater in carnal form and worldly appearance than ever had been the case with fallen Israel.

Under this coming apostasy the spiritual and heavenly remnant, cleaving to the testimony, would be persecuted, swamped, and often overwhelmed. Again, this would exceed the case in Israel of the remnant according to the election of grace regarded as the outcasts of Israel by the great professing body of the Jews.

It was this falling away of Israel as a whole that had brought upon the nation those fearful woes and perpetual destructions under which the wrath of God should abide upon them.

That day of wrath and judgment will be as sudden and unexpected as was that of the flood in the days of Noah. The judgment will be as inexorable, falling upon every faithless servant. Of the ten virgins, the folly of five will exclude them.

Of all the flock, not one of the goats shall escape that judgment which is according to works, despite their convictions to the contrary, and for all their loud and loving profession of Christ.

Every one of these shall go away into everlasting punishment. But the righteous—*for that is the character of the sheep*—shall enter into life eternal.

Matthew now narrates the eighth division of this gospel:

The Betrayal of Messiah and the Kingdom, Chapter 26

Events crowd one upon the other in succession. This was the beginning of the end. The assembly of the wicked, the council of the Jews, determine to put Jesus to death. But they did not know, nor could they see, the determinate counsel and foreknowledge of God to appoint their rebellion to achieve his own predestined purpose.

According to this means, Christ would abolish in his flesh the enmity, even the law of commandments contained in ordinances, for to make in himself of twain, Jew and Gentile, one new man, so making peace. He would reconcile both—called out of the Jews and from the Gentiles—unto God in one body by the cross, slaying the enmity thereby.

However, the remaining chapters are not doctrinal: they are the historical record of unfolding events. Before the end we see two estimates of the value of Jesus: one out of the house of a poor leper, by a woman of dubious repute; the other from one of the twelve, with the chief priests of all Israel.

One amounted to a great sum, the outpouring of a fortune. The other totalled thirty pieces of silver, the miserable price of a slave, according to the lowest estimation of the law.

On the fourteenth day of the first month in Israel, the first day of unleavened bread, when the passover must be killed and eaten, the Jews were absorbed with the performance of this annual religious and ceremonial ritual.

Meanwhile the Lamb of God, the Christ, the true Passover—whom the sacrificial ceremony foreshadowed—went unnoticed. Instead, he was betrayed by an apostle; denied by the chiefest disciple; forsaken of his own; and condemned by the Jews on a false pretext at an unlawful assembly, to be delivered to the Gentiles to be crucified.

But first 'On the night in which he was betrayed' Matthew records the last supper, following the eating of the passover in the place appointed. Here the first evangelist gives the historical narrative of a single event which took place, an event figurative of Jesus' coming death, without the least hint of a commemorative re-enactment regularly to be repeated by the *ecclesia* in the future.

Matthew says nothing whatsoever of remembrance. In this gospel—the *ecclesia* gospel, note—the supper took place: this was what took place; and it was all that took place.

They sung a psalm, and went out into the mount of Olives. Then Jesus foretold 'All ye shall be offended because of me this night: for it is written, I will smite the shepherd, and the sheep of the flock shall be scattered abroad. But after I am risen again, I will go before you into Galilee.'

Peter could not bear the suggestion that he should be thought capable of such an offence. However in answer Jesus prophesied of Peter's threefold denial before cock-crow in the morning.

There follows Jesus' agony in the garden of Gethsemane, his soul being sorrowful and very heavy. Three times he left Peter and the two sons of Zebedee, going forward to fall on his face, crying to the Father that if it were possible this cup might pass from him, his soul exceedingly sorrowful, even unto death. Three times he returned to the disciples and found them asleep, their eyes being heavy.

The third time all was settled. They might sleep on now, and take their rest. Nevertheless, said Jesus, they should rise and go hence, for the hour was come.

While Jesus yet spake these words, Judas came with a great multitude, having swords and staves, to betray the Son of man with a kiss. Jesus was taken. A feeble intervention with a sword followed, which Christ prevented, prophesying again, The scripture must be fulfilled, that thus it must be. For all this was done, that the scriptures of the prophets might come to pass.

Jesus' disciples forsook him, and fled.

He was taken and led away to the palace of Caiaphas the high priest, where the scribes and elders were assembled. By false witness, knowingly contrived, Jesus was condemned. He was unlawfully beaten in the sight of all the highest assembly of the rulers and the whole council of the Jews.

Meanwhile Peter denied him thrice, yet only in order to stay by him. But the cock crew. He went out, and wept bitterly.

Matthew continues the narrative:

The Condemnation of Messiah and the Kingdom, Chapter 27

Although the events of this, the ninth distinct division of Matthew, take place on the day following the Betrayal—the previous division—yet in Jewish terms it was *still* the first day of unleavened bread, the day on which they kill the passover.

The reason for this lies in the fact that—to the Jew—the day is considered to run *from evening to evening.* Hence the first day of unleavened bread *began* in terms of Jewish reckoning *on the previous evening*, and would not end until the *next* evening, by which time Jesus would be crucified, dead, and buried.

This simple observation resolves the apparent difficulty arising from the truth that Jesus was crucified, slain, and buried on the sixth day—the so-called Friday—that his dead body lay in the tomb on the seventh—sabbath—day, and that he arose very early on the next day, that is, the following first day of the week.

This seems to total only two days, and yet Jesus is said to have lain three days in the grave. Once one counts the days by Jewish reckoning—evening to evening—and not by western chronology, this is exactly correct: he rose on the third day.

The first day of the feast of unleavened bread was distinguished by putting away leaven from every Jewish household.

But why? Because—unrealized by the Jews, blind to anything but the form and ceremony—leaven was the *figure* of inbred sin, in its presence, its permeation, and its fermenting motions. Leaven worked within the loaf to cause the whole to swell in the heat of the oven. So it is with the working of inbred sin in the soul and body of this corruption.

Yet on what occasion was the inward working of that which leaven *typified*—the motions of sin—stronger than at this particular Passover? Whenever was the figurative meaning of the feast of unleavened bread more contradicted than when the punctilious Jews made such a show of avoiding the least appearance of the form whilst displaying the greatest exhibition of the reality?

The Jews were never so full of that which leaven signified. The whole was leavened. Inbred sin in the religious was at its uttermost fulness and greatest heat in the day of the betrayal and condemnation of Messiah and the kingdom.

Yet hiding behind the performance of the outward form and ceremony, the Jews shielded their eyes from the worst evil ever committed upon the face of the earth since time began. But no defiling leaven; O no: that be far from them.

Never in the course of human history was mankind more conspicuous in the display of the working of all that leaven typified. Never at any time was inbred sin stronger than on the day of the crucifixion. Yet never since Adam was formed from the dust of the ground was a people seen to be so full of outward form, ceremony, and appearance of religious duty.

Never had Israel been under such light as that which radiated from the presence of David's Lord and Abraham's Seed, the Messiah, the King of the Jews, the Light of the world, the Son of man and Son of God, standing before their very faces.

Never, no, never was what leaven *signified* more evident in its inward malice and enmity, its interior swelling and tumultuous motion, than on that day when for form and ceremony's sake—wherein the Jews trusted for righteousness before God—not a tincture of leaven *itself* was to be found throughout all the dwellings of Israel.

The chief priests and elders of the people took counsel to put Jesus to death, delivering him to the Gentiles, as he himself had prophesied. Judas, full of remorse at the consequences of his betrayal—consequences which he had never expected—repents, protesting Jesus' innocence. He casts down the pieces of silver in the temple.

But neither God nor men would receive either repentance or restitution. Yet what Judas did in penance was the epitome of the supposedly infallible prescription of such as J. Wesley, C.G. Finney, and the Arminian host, in order to bargain a pardon from the Almighty. Judas—one of the twelve—knew better by experience and judgment, and went and hanged himself, irredeemably lost for time and eternity.

Jesus having been delivered up to the Gentiles, the governor, Pilate, finds no fault in him, though much with the Jews. He labours to acquit their Messiah, on no higher ground than common Roman justice. But the Jews ensnare the governor with such guile that Pilate's sense of self-preservation prevailed against his effort to uphold the common justice which he was sworn to preserve.

Pilate made one last attempt to circumvent the rulers of the Jews, by appealing over their heads to the people. But the nation of Israel accepted the guilt of Jesus' murder, in their name, and in that of their posterity, condemning the Messiah and rejecting the kingdom. Pilate would do no more.

Jesus was scourged—or flogged: it is the word 'flagellate'—then mocked, and finally led away to be crucified. They gave him vinegar to drink, mingled with gall. He refused to drink. They crucified him. The soldiers parted his garments, and cast lots for his vesture. They watched him. Over his head his accusation was written: THIS IS JESUS, THE KING OF THE JEWS.

But it was not an accusation: it was a matter of fact. In fact they condemned their Messiah, and rejected his kingdom, because he *was* their Messiah, and it *was* the kingdom. But they had cried out the more saying 'Let him be crucified'.

Pilate, washing his hands before the multitude, had replied, 'I am innocent of the blood of this just person: see ye to it. Then answered all the people, and said, His blood be on us, and on our children.' It was on this ground that Pilate commanded the crucifixion, and wrote the superscription.

They that passed by reviled Jesus, wagging their heads, unknowingly using the words of the temptation: 'If thou be the Son of God.' The chief priests, with the scribes and elders, make the journey to mock also, appealing to Jesus' past words, deeds, and miracles, as the basis of his delivering himself.

Thus they confessed their full awareness of his entire ministry, besides the unique signs and wonders by which God testified to the Messiah and the kingdom. The thieves crucified with him likewise cast the same in his teeth.

Now from the sixth hour there was darkness over all the land until the ninth hour. The world was in darkness. About the ninth hour Jesus cried with a loud voice, 'Eli, Eli, lama sabachthani? that is to say, My God, my God, why hast thou forsaken me?'

These were the opening words of David in the twenty-second psalm, a psalm figurative of the sufferings of Christ, written in prophecy when David was outcast, hounded, and persecuted by the rulers and people of Israel.

But now the type was fulfilled, and the prophecy accomplished. The bystanders misunderstood the words which Jesus spoke, just as they could not see the death he was dying. Jesus cried the second time with a loud voice, and yielded up the ghost.

Forthwith the veil of the temple was rent in twain from the top to the bottom; the earth did quake; the rocks rent; and the graves were opened. Three days later, after Jesus had risen, many *bodies* of the saints arose from the opened graves, and went unto the holy city, and appeared unto many.

The centurion, and the Gentiles that were with him, watching Jesus, when they saw the earthquake, and the things which were accomplished, did what the Jews did not: they feared greatly, and said, 'Truly this was the Son of God.' Nevertheless a remnant, especially women, beholding afar off, feared also.

Joseph of Arimathea, a great man of wealth, pleaded with Pilate for the body of Jesus, that it might lie in his own new tomb. Thus Jesus' grave was made with the rich in his death. The dead body was laid to rest in Joseph's sepulchre.

But now the evening drew on, when the sabbath would begin. No work, no embalming, could commence until the following first day of the week. For this, the embalmers waited.

The next day the chief priests and Pharisees had no sabbatical scruples about coming to Pilate that he might enforce the power of Rome. So well did they know the words and deeds of Jesus, that, having mocked him with both at the cross, now they concern themselves with the resurrection of which he had prophesied.

They conjecture that the prophecy of Jesus' rising again was a plan devised beforehand, in which his disciples should steal away the body on the third day in order to give an appearance of resurrection. To make this impossible to achieve, the chief priests and Pharisees craved the might of Rome to protect the dead body.

Troops are dispatched to keep guard over the sepulchre continually. The watch is to stand both day and night. Masons are to enclose the tomb. The imperial seal is to be affixed across the secured entrance.

The military power of the greatest empire the world had ever seen forbad both entry or exit. And the rulers of the strictest form of outward religion to which this world would ever rise sat back satisfied, at last able to rest in what was left of the sabbath day. The thing was over. Sealed.

That was the end. So concluded the world power, and the powers of religion. Their exclusion of the Messiah and the kingdom was safeguarded. Religion rested safely where they considered it belonged: in their own hands.

Finally the tenth division of the Gospel according to Matthew—again, so obviously and naturally a division in and of itself—concludes the narrative:

The Justification of Messiah and the Kingdom, Chapter 28

The chapter opens 'In the end of the sabbath'. The sabbath, or seventh, day was that in which 'God ended his work which he had made; and he rested on the seventh day from all his work which he had made', Gen. 2:2.

He made the heavens and all the host of them; he made the earth, the sea, the dry land; he made the grass of the field, the trees of the wood; he made the fish of the sea, every creeping thing, the fowls of the air, and the beasts of the field. Finally, he made man: male and female created he them.

And God saw everything that he had made, and, behold, it was very good. And the evening and the morning were the sixth day. On the seventh day, the sabbath day, he rested. He was at rest in his creation, and in the man whom he had set over all.

Now no more. Since the Fall, God has found, and can find, no cause of rest, either in creation or in man. The sabbath day became merely symbolical and typical: it ceased to indicate God resting in his creation. In his very nature, he *cannot* rest in fallen creation. Even as the Messiah said when he wrought —not rested—on the sabbath day, 'My Father *worketh* hitherto, and I *work*.'

Although God *had* rested on the seventh day of creation, after the Fall of man he rested therein no longer. Then, the sabbath was but a figure. But he does not rest in figures, but in the true. Not in the shadow, but in the substance. He rests in Christ, not Adam. He rests in the work of Christ, not the transgression of Adam. He rests in the inheritance of Christ, he has no rest in this present age.

In his divine foreknowledge, this rest of God in Christ and the kingdom of heaven is that which the sabbath typified from the very beginning. But the Fall of man brought to an end all divine rest in anything at all pertaining to the creation of this world, the creation of man, or anything generated in succession from fallen man or from the creature.

Indeed, the Fall of man brought to an end God's rest in anything throughout the unbroken ages of time till the day of judgment. He has no peace in it, and it has nothing but enmity to him.

God's rest appeared at last in the Messiah and the kingdom. This the holy prophets had foretold from the foundation of the world. But the Jews crucified the Messiah, and rejected the kingdom. They buried him, sealed the tomb, and kept their watch with all the power of Rome and all the malevolence of religion. Then they kept *their* sabbath.

'In the end of the sabbath', Mt. 28:1. Thus even the type itself is ended. This is the *end.* There never was, and there never will be any rest in this present creation, or in the world that now is, or in its religion, or in the first man. The heavens and earth that are now, by the word of God are kept in store, reserved unto fire against the judgment and perdition of ungodly men, II Peter 3:7.

God has no rest in anything under heaven, upon earth, or in time. He has no rest in man, or in the generation of Adam, whether Jew or Gentile. This is that generation which crucified the Messiah and rejected the kingdom.

But the Son arose on another day. A new day. The first day. There is a new creation. 'This is the day which the LORD hath made; we will rejoice and be glad in it', Ps. 118:24.

Day unto day uttereth speech, and the speech of the Lord's day, which commenced with the ascension of the Son into the heavens, continues with his reign, and ends with his return, the speech, I say, is that of peace, and of peace in the rest that remains for the people of God.

In this day of the Lord, the light is separated from the darkness, and the light of the Son streams constantly and inwardly from above: there is no night there. In this continuous spiritual day all things are become new, and all that is new shall and must be ushered in by Christ in the new testament.

This is manifested experimentally by bitter disillusionment with the old, and heartfelt hope in the new; 'Came Mary

Magdalene and the other Mary to the sepulchre', Mt. 28:1. The name Mary is derived from the Hebrew 'Mara'.

This is the name which Naomi took to herself on her return from the land of Moab, Ruth 1:20-22. The Hebrew signifies 'bitterness'. 'Call me not Naomi, call me Mara: for the Almighty hath dealt very bitterly with me', Ruth 1:20.

Bitter disappointment, bitter disillusionment, with the old. No rest. Hence, in the testimony of the godly women, the two 'Marys', it is 'the *end* of the sabbath'. All their hope lay in the sepulchre, with its promise of a better resurrection. All their faith rested in the God of glory, by whom 'Women received their dead to life again'. All their love lingered over the dead body in the tomb, awaiting 'the first day of the week'.

'Mary'—'Mara'—the name shared by the two women, bears witness to their common experience of bitterness wrought of God in the inward soul—'for the *Almighty* hath dealt very bitterly with me'—under law; in the world; through life: all was found to be a barren wilderness, bitter and dry, lifeless and hostile.

This divinely taught bitterness—'And they shall be all taught of God', Jn. 6:45—is the experience that *must* precede any true coming to Messiah. This is to be taught of the Father: 'Every one that hath heard, and learned of the Father, cometh unto me', Jn. 6:45.

'He will teach sinners in the way', Ps. 25:8. Teach them what? That everything, but everything, from Adam, on earth, from the world, under Moses, is *nothing but unendurable bitterness*. 'Blessed is the man whom thou chastenest, O LORD, and teachest him *out of thy law*', Ps. 94:12. This is bitter teaching; bitter law-work. But it does lead, and it must lead, to the sweetness of Christ: 'Weeping may endure for a night, but joy cometh in the morning', Ps. 30:5. The morning, spiritually, dawns with the rising of the Son. 'Who teacheth like him?', Job 36:22.

Such divine and experimental teaching, such interior discipline, the two 'Maras' signify. None other come to Christ, nor can come to Christ. But these come, for to them there is nothing *but* Christ, in heaven, on earth; in time, for eternity; through life, in death; out of the grave, in the resurrection.

When thus taught, one is left dead to the flesh, crucified to the world, and mortified to every worldly pleasure, shut up to faith: *Then* Christ is all. Not before. He is All in All to none but the Bride. And this, the two women typify: a twofold witness to the Bride.

As Eve was formed out of Adam, so a suited Bride—in a mystery—was predestined to be taken out of the side of the Messiah, the Son of God, the Last Adam, the Second Man, in the deep sleep of his death on the cross. Now, risen, Christ foresees that Bride in a figure presented to him by his Father, in the greeting of the two Marys, and in the prospect of the glorious inheritance of the world to come.

Matthew records—what neither Mark, Luke, nor John mention—'Behold, there was a great earthquake', Mt. 28:2.

In each Evangelist's account of these very crowded events, persons, and visions—sometimes the same persons active again after only a short interval—there is a fine discrimination. Only in Matthew does the doctrine necessitate the Spirit's testimony of the descent from heaven of the angel of the Lord, whose countenance was as lightning, and raiment white as snow, for fear of whom 'the keepers became as dead men'.

And for fear of the *great* earthquake. This premonition of the uneasy earth indicated a kind of apprehension of the coming end of the world, the harbinger of which was signified by the quaking of the earth.

The very globe trembled before the certainty of the dissolution of all things at the judgment, testified by the death, burial and resurrection of Messiah, heir of the world *to come*. That is, to come at the general resurrection, at the end of time, at the conflagration of *this* world.

The resurrection of the just, however, is destined not for this world, but for that world to come, whereof we speak. This is risen Messiah's inheritance with his disciples. The world saw it, and trembled; the earth beheld, and quaked. Hence the account of the 'great earthquake', limited to Matthew, bears directly on the record of Messiah and the kingdom, to complement the doctrine as the whole.

With the earthquake, the descent of the angel, and the rolling away of the stone, came the announcement *that the tomb was already empty*. 'He is *not here*.' 'Go quickly: tell his disciples that he is risen from the dead; and, behold, he goeth before you into Galilee; there shall ye see him: lo, I have told you', Mt. 28:2-7.

Jesus *had* risen, and risen bodily, passing through all obstacles, every impediment, leaving each one undisturbed and intact, with the watch secure in the false assurance that nothing had taken place, or could have escaped their vigilance.

However, by this time, God had finished his work. That is, the work of a new creation in Christ. Nevertheless men were oblivious of everything. Not so the two Marys. Bitter as to this world, themselves, and the flesh, they showed forth every feminine instinct, borne of love to the Messiah. Meek, sensitive, intuitive, submissive, apprehensive of his presence: here was the figure of the Bride, with a twofold witness.

As they ran to the disciples with the angelic message that Jesus would meet them in Galilee, their very haste manifested that engagement to Christ which rose over each earthly affection, every self-interest, and all the allurement of this present world. Hurrying on their way, 'Lo, Jesus met them, saying, All hail. And they came and held him by the feet, and worshipped him', Mt. 28:9.

The Son of God, risen bodily from the dead, not only manifested himself to the two Marys, but also adds to the message given by the angel, saying, 'Be not afraid: go tell my brethren, that they go into Galilee, and there shall they see me', Mt. 28:10. Go tell *my brethren.* Not, as the angel, *his disciples.* The Messiah reserves to himself the saying, '*My brethren*'.

If *his brethren*, then sons of his Father. Hence, through death, by resurrection, in union, *sonship* had been effected, and the kingdom realized in life begotten from heaven above. Nothing but darkness and death reigned on the earth below. Jerusalem, the circumcision, all that stood in earthly Israel, all that obtained under law, the world itself, in the counsel of God had been brought down to the grave in judgment at the cross.

But *his brethren* are not of earthly Jerusalem, not of Israel after the flesh, not of this world, not of darkness: they *have* passed from death unto life, Jn. 5:24.

His brethren are found in Galilee, where nothing signifies save Messiah and the kingdom. Nothing is *there* save Messiah and the kingdom. Galilee of the Gentiles: a place far separate from the earthly system of religion denominated by the epithet *Jerusalem below*, which abides in darkness and is under the curse.

The religious leaders of that 'Jerusalem below' had entreated Pilate, 'Sir, we remember that that deceiver said, while he was yet alive, After three days I will rise again. Command therefore that the sepulchre be made sure until the third day, lest his disciples come by night, and steal him away, and say unto the people, He is risen from the dead: so the last error shall be worse than the first', Mt. 27:63,64.

Deceiver? Disciples? Stealing the body? Creeping about at night? What? None but two meek women drew near the sepulchre in Matthew, and at that, only at daybreak.

And do the Jews need an entire armed watch, a whole troop of soldiers, to keep at bay two mild and gentle women? In full daylight? For it is certain that no others drew near in Matthew, much less by night. Then why this armed watch? Why the troop of soldiers? To save themselves from two women in full daylight? As the Lord liveth, he that sitteth in the heavens shall laugh: the LORD shall have them in derision.

In Matthew but two feeble women drew near. As to the Jews, in the teeth of all their contrivance; by incontrovertible evidence; by the testimony of the entire watch; by the attestation of heaven; by the witness of the angel of the Lord: the resurrection was verified beyond all doubt, being confirmed by the mouth of the Jews' own allies, the representatives of the might of imperial Rome.

Yet manifesting the blind enmity of earthly religion revealed throughout Matthew, the Jews expose their madness to the full: they bribe the soldiers to lie in their teeth, overcoming their fear of their superior officers—and of the governor—by the huge sum of money offered.

Money? Whence this money? Money entrusted to the custodians of the temple, given by the people to the LORD, laid up in the treasury? And will they use this money to bribe the Gentiles to lie, deliberately blinding the eyes of the people to the truth?

Thus by the Jews' deceit the lie spread apace: that his disciples had stolen away the body. And hence through their bribery—misusing temple money—the lie remained uncontradicted by the soldiers whom the religious leaders had corrupted through covetousness, Mt. 28:12 to 15.

However, on the testimony of the two Marys—in Matthew—the eleven go to the mountain which Jesus had appointed in Galilee. Far beyond the land of Israel, in Galilee of the Gentiles, they meet Jesus on that elevation over Jerusalem below, where the Son reveals himself in the glory of Jerusalem above.

They saw him. They worshipped him. But some doubted. Are these the doubters conspicuous by their absence in the Acts and the epistles? Some—not one, not two: some—out of no more than eleven, *some* doubted.

But nothing will, and nothing can, prevent the Lord in his purpose. He sends forth the believing disciples, all power being given unto him in heaven and in earth. Here they are not called apostles: 'disciples' is the word, just as teaching is the function, and all nations the suited sphere.

The disciples, also called brethren, are no longer seen in connection with Israel, Jerusalem below, or an earthly inheritance; neither is theirs a worldly sanctuary, a carnal priesthood, a legal rule, or a repetitive sacrifice. To all this they have been crucified with Christ once and for all.

The resurrection was manifested in Galilee, where nothing but Christ prevailed to draw and unite the disciples. They are viewed as one in Father, Son, and Holy Ghost, commanded by the risen Son to 'Go therefore, and teach all nations, baptizing them in the name of the Father, and of the Son, and of the Holy Ghost: teaching them to observe all things whatsoever I have commanded you.'

The disciples go forth as 'brethren', and if so, as the sons of God, in union with Christ, having been received into the kingdom of heaven. They are to preach and teach the testimony of Jesus recorded throughout the Gospel according to Matthew. They are sent to make disciples of all nations, 'Teaching them to observe all things whatsoever I have commanded you.'

If so, at this very moment, to this present hour, now, today, so long as time shall last, and the age shall stand, 'Lo, I am with you alway, even unto the end of the world. Amen.'

Wherever he sends; in all places to which the disciples are directed; no matter what the consequences: 'I am with you'—note that it is 'you', plural; not 'thee', singular—'alway, even unto the end of the world.' This cannot, in the nature of things it cannot, be confined to the first disciples. Two thousand years might have passed. Yes, but the end of the age has not yet come.

He is with *you*, called, taught, commanded, and sent, today, now, even unto the *end* of the age. If some doubt now, some doubted then. And if it made no difference then, why should it make any difference now?

Still the enlightened eyes of called, prepared, taught, and sent disciples are to be fixed upon the spiritually present Messiah, in the very midst, preaching this same kingdom of heaven. 'And, lo, I am with you *alway*, even unto the end of the age.' Amen, and Amen.

JOHN METCALFE

INDEX

TO OTHER PUBLICATIONS

PSALMS, HYMNS AND SPIRITUAL SONGS

THE PSALMS

OF THE

OLD TESTAMENT

The Psalms of the Old Testament, the result of years of painstaking labour, is an original translation into verse from the Authorised Version, which seeks to present the Psalms in the purest scriptural form possible for singing. Here, for the first time, divine names are rendered as and when they occur in the scripture, the distinction between LORD and Lord has been preserved, and every essential point of doctrine and experience appears with unique perception and fidelity.

The Psalms of the Old Testament is the first part of a trilogy written by John Metcalfe, the second part of which is entitled *Spiritual Songs from the Gospels*, and the last, *The Hymns of the New Testament*. These titles provide unique and accurate metrical versions of passages from the psalms, the gospels and the new testament epistles respectively, and are intended to be used together in the worship of God.

Price £2.50 *(postage extra)*
(hard-case binding, dust-jacket)
Printed, sewn and bound
by the John Metcalfe Publishing Trust
ISBN 0 9506366 7 3

SPIRITUAL SONGS
FROM
THE GOSPELS

The *Spiritual Songs from the Gospels*, the result of years of painstaking labour, is an original translation into verse from the Authorised Version, which seeks to present essential parts of the gospels in the purest scriptural form possible for singing. The careful selection from Matthew, Mark, Luke and John, set forth in metrical verse of the highest integrity, enables the singer to sing 'the word of Christ' as if from the scripture itself, 'richly and in all wisdom'; and, above all, in a way that facilitates worship in song of unprecedented fidelity.

The *Spiritual Songs from the Gospels* is the central part of a trilogy written by John Metcalfe, the first part of which is entitled *The Psalms of the Old Testament*, and the last, *The Hymns of the New Testament*. These titles provide unique and accurate metrical versions of passages from the psalms, the gospels and the new testament epistles respectively, and are intended to be used together in the worship of God.

Price £2.50 *(postage extra)*
(hard-case binding, dust-jacket)
Printed, sewn and bound
by the John Metcalfe Publishing Trust
ISBN 0 9506366 8 1

THE HYMNS
OF THE
NEW TESTAMENT

The *Hymns of the New Testament*, the result of years of painstaking labour, is an original translation into verse from the Authorised Version, which presents essential parts of the new testament epistles in the purest scriptural form possible for singing. The careful selection from the book of Acts to that of Revelation, set forth in metrical verse of the highest integrity, enables the singer to sing 'the word of Christ' as if from the scripture itself, 'richly and in all wisdom'; and, above all, in a way that facilitates worship in song of unprecedented fidelity.

The *Hymns of the New Testament* is the last part of a trilogy written by John Metcalfe, the first part of which is entitled *The Psalms of the Old Testament*, and the next, *Spiritual Songs from the Gospels.* These titles provide unique and accurate metrical versions of passages from the psalms, the gospels and the new testament epistles respectively, and are intended to be used together in the worship of God.

Price £2.50 *(postage extra)*
(hard-case binding, dust-jacket)
Printed, sewn and bound
by the John Metcalfe Publishing Trust
ISBN 0 9506366 9 X

'THE APOSTOLIC FOUNDATION OF THE CHRISTIAN CHURCH' SERIES

Third Printing

FOUNDATIONS UNCOVERED

THE APOSTOLIC FOUNDATION
OF THE
CHRISTIAN CHURCH

Volume I

Foundations Uncovered is the introduction to the major series: 'The Apostolic Foundation of the Christian Church'.

Rich in truth, the Introduction deals comprehensively with the foundation of the apostolic faith under the descriptive titles: The Word, The Doctrine, The Truth, The Gospel, The Faith, The New Testament, and The Foundation.

The contents of the book reveal: The Fact of the Foundation; The Foundation Uncovered; What the Foundation is not; How the Foundation is Described; and, Being Built upon the Foundation.

'This book comes with the freshness of a new Reformation.'

Price 75p *(postage extra)*
(Laminated cover)
Printed, sewn and bound
by the John Metcalfe Publishing Trust
ISBN 0 9506366 5 7

Thoroughly revised and extensively rewritten second edition

Third Printing

THE BIRTH OF JESUS CHRIST

THE APOSTOLIC FOUNDATION OF THE CHRISTIAN CHURCH

Volume II

'The very spirit of adoration and worship rings through the pages of *The Birth of Jesus Christ*.

'The author expresses with great clarity the truths revealed to him in his study of holy scriptures at depth. We are presented here with a totally lofty view of the Incarnation.

'John Metcalfe is to be classed amongst the foremost expositors of our age; and his writings have about them that quality of timelessness that makes me sure they will one day take their place among the heritage of truly great Christian works.'

From a review by Rev. David Catterson.

'Uncompromisingly faithful to scripture ... has much to offer which is worth serious consideration ... deeply moving.'

The Expository Times.

Price 95p *(postage extra)*
(Laminated Cover)
Printed, sewn and bound
by the John Metcalfe Publishing Trust
ISBN 1 870039 48 3

Thoroughly revised and extensively rewritten
second edition

Third Printing

THE MESSIAH

THE APOSTOLIC FOUNDATION
OF THE
CHRISTIAN CHURCH

Volume III

The Messiah is a spiritually penetrating and entirely original exposition of Matthew chapter one to chapter seven from the trenchant pen of John Metcalfe.

Matthew Chapters One to Seven

GENEALOGY · BIRTH · STAR OF BETHLEHEM
HEROD · FLIGHT TO EGYPT · NAZARETH
JOHN THE BAPTIST · THE BAPTIST'S MINISTRY
JESUS' BAPTISM · ALL RIGHTEOUSNESS FULFILLED
HEAVEN OPENED · THE SPIRIT'S DESCENT
THE TEMPTATION OF JESUS IN THE WILDERNESS
JESUS' MANIFESTATION · THE CALLING · THE TRUE DISCIPLES
THE BEATITUDES · THE SERMON ON THE MOUNT

'Something of the fire of the ancient Hebrew prophet .... Metcalfe has spiritual and expository potentials of a high order.'

The Life of Faith.

Price £7.75 *(postage extra)*
Hardback 420 pages
Laminated bookjacket
Printed, sewn and bound
by the John Metcalfe Publishing Trust
ISBN 1 870039 51 3

THE SON OF GOD AND SEED OF DAVID

THE APOSTOLIC FOUNDATION
OF THE
CHRISTIAN CHURCH

Volume IV

The Son of God and Seed of David is the fourth volume in the major work entitled 'The Apostolic Foundation of the Christian Church.'

'The author proceeds to open and allege that Jesus Christ is and ever was *The Son of God*. This greatest of subjects, this most profound of all mysteries, is handled with reverence and with outstanding perception.

'The second part considers *The Seed of David*. What is meant precisely by 'the seed'? And why 'of David'? With prophetic insight the author expounds these essential verities.'

Price £6.95 *(postage extra)*
Hardback 250 pages
Laminated bookjacket
Printed, sewn and bound
by the John Metcalfe Publishing Trust
ISBN 1 870039 16 5

CHRIST CRUCIFIED

THE APOSTOLIC FOUNDATION
OF THE
CHRISTIAN CHURCH

Volume V

Christ Crucified the definitive work on the crucifixion, the blood, and the cross of Jesus Christ.

The crucifixion of Jesus Christ witnessed in the Gospels: the gospel according to Matthew; Mark; Luke; John.

The blood of Jesus Christ declared in the Epistles: the shed blood; the blood of purchase; redemption through his blood; the blood of sprinkling; the blood of the covenant.

The doctrine of the cross revealed in the apostolic foundation of the Christian church: the doctrine of the cross; the cross and the body of sin; the cross and the carnal mind; the cross and the law; the offence of the cross; the cross of our Lord Jesus Christ.

Price £6.95 *(postage extra)*
Hardback 300 pages
Laminated bookjacket
Printed, sewn and bound
by the John Metcalfe Publishing Trust
ISBN 1 870039 08 4

JUSTIFICATION BY FAITH

THE APOSTOLIC FOUNDATION
OF THE
CHRISTIAN CHURCH

Volume VI

THE HEART OF THE GOSPEL · THE FOUNDATION OF THE CHURCH
THE ISSUE OF ETERNITY
CLEARLY, ORIGINALLY AND POWERFULLY OPENED

The basis · The righteousness of the law
The righteousness of God · The atonement · Justification
Traditional views considered · Righteousness imputed to faith
Faith counted for righteousness · Justification by Faith

'And it came to pass, when Jesus had ended these sayings, the people were astonished at his doctrine: for he taught them as one having authority, and not as the scribes.' Matthew 7:28,29.

Price £7.50 *(postage extra)*
Hardback 375 pages
Laminated bookjacket
Printed, sewn and bound
by the John Metcalfe Publishing Trust
ISBN 1870039 11 4

THE CHURCH: WHAT IS IT?

THE APOSTOLIC FOUNDATION
OF THE
CHRISTIAN CHURCH

Volume VII

The answer to this question proceeds first from the lips of Jesus himself, Mt. 16:18, later to be expounded by the words of the apostles whom he sent.

Neither fear of man nor favour from the world remotely affect the answer.

Here is the truth, the whole truth, and nothing but the truth.

The complete originality, the vast range, and the total fearlessness of this book command the attention in a way that is unique.

Read this book: you will never read another like it.

Outspokenly devastating yet devastatingly constructive.

Price £7.75 *(postage extra)*
Hardback 400 pages
Laminated bookjacket
Printed, sewn and bound
by the John Metcalfe Publishing Trust
ISBN 1 870039 23 8

OTHER TITLES

NOAH AND THE FLOOD

Noah and the Flood expounds with vital urgency the man and the message that heralded the end of the old world. The description of the flood itself is vividly realistic. The whole work has an unmistakable ring of authority, and speaks as 'Thus saith the Lord'.

'Mr. Metcalfe makes a skilful use of persuasive eloquence as he challenges the reality of one's profession of faith ... he gives a rousing call to a searching self-examination and evaluation of one's spiritual experience.'

The Monthly Record of the Free Church of Scotland.

Price £1.90 *(postage extra)*
(Laminated Cover)
Printed, sewn and bound
by the John Metcalfe Publishing Trust
ISBN 1 870039 22 X

DIVINE FOOTSTEPS

Divine Footsteps traces the pathway of the feet of the Son of man from the very beginning in the prophetic figures of the true in the old testament through the reality in the new; doing so in a way of experimental spirituality. At the last a glimpse of the coming glory is beheld as his feet are viewed as standing at the latter day upon the earth.

Price 95p *(postage extra)*
(Laminated Cover)
Printed, sewn and bound
by the John Metcalfe Publishing Trust
ISBN 1 870039 21 1

THE RED HEIFER

The Red Heifer was the name given to a sacrifice used by the children of Israel in the Old Testament—as recorded in Numbers 19—in which a heifer was slain and burned. Cedar wood, hyssop and scarlet were cast into the burning, and the ashes were mingled with running water and put in a vessel. It was kept for the children of Israel for a water of separation: it was a purification for sin.

In this unusual book the sacrifice is brought up to date and its relevance to the church today is shown.

Price 75p *(postage extra)*
ISBN 0 9502515 4 2

THE WELLS OF SALVATION

The Wells of Salvation is written from a series of seven powerful addresses preached at Tylers Green. It is a forthright and experimental exposition of Isaiah 12:3, 'Therefore with joy shall ye draw water out of the wells of salvation.'

John Metcalfe is acknowledged to be perhaps the most gifted expositor and powerful preacher of our day and this is to be seen clearly in The Wells of Salvation.

Price £1.50 *(postage extra)*
(Laminated Cover)
ISBN 0 9502515 6 9

OF GOD OR MAN?

LIGHT FROM GALATIANS

The Epistle to the Galatians contends for deliverance from the law and from carnal ministry.

The Apostle opens his matter in two ways:

Firstly, Paul vindicates himself and his ministry against those that came not from God above, but from Jerusalem below.

Secondly, he defends the Gospel and evangelical liberty against legal perversions and bondage to the flesh.

Price £1.45 *(postage extra)*
(Laminated Cover)
ISBN 0 9506366 3 0

A QUESTION FOR POPE JOHN PAUL II

As a consequence of his many years spent apart in prayer, lonely vigil, and painstaking study of the scripture, John Metcalfe asks a question and looks for an answer from Pope John Paul II.

Price £1.25. *(postage extra)*
(Laminated Cover)
ISBN 0 9506366 4 9

THE BOOK OF RUTH

The Book of Ruth is set against the farming background of old testament Israel at the time of the Judges, the narrative—unfolding the work of God in redemption—being marked by a series of agricultural events.

These events—the famine; the barley harvest; the wheat harvest; the winnowing—possessed a hidden spiritual significance to that community, but, much more, they speak in figure directly to our own times, as the book reveals.

Equally contemporary appear the characters of Ruth, Naomi, Boaz, and the first kinsman, drawn with spiritual perception greatly to the profit of the reader.

Price £4.95 *(postage extra)*
Hardback 200 pages
Laminated bookjacket
Printed, sewn and bound
by the John Metcalfe Publishing Trust
ISBN 1 870039 17 3

PRESENT-DAY CONVERSIONS
OF THE NEW TESTAMENT KIND

FROM THE MINISTRY OF

JOHN METCALFE

The outstandingly striking presentation of this fascinating paperback will surely catch the eye, as its title and contents will certainly captivate the mind: here is a unique publication.

Woven into a gripping narrative, over twenty-one short life stories, all centred on conversions that simply could not have happened had not God broken in, and had not Christ been revealed, the book presents a tremendous challenge, at once moving and thrilling to the reader.

Price £2.25 *(postage extra)*
(Laminated Cover)
Printed, sewn and bound
by the John Metcalfe Publishing Trust
ISBN 1 870039 31 9

DIVINE MEDITATIONS

OF

WILLIAM HUNTINGTON

Originally published by Mr. Huntington as a series of letters to J. Jenkins, under the title of 'Contemplations on the God of Israel', the spiritual content of this correspondence has been skilfully and sympathetically edited, abridged, and arranged so as to form a series of meditations, suitable for daily readings.

Mr. Huntington's own text is thereby adapted to speak directly to the reader in a way much more suited to his ministering immediately to ourselves, in our own circumstances and times.

It is greatly hoped that many today will benefit from this adaption which carefully retains both the spirit and the letter of the text. If any prefer the original format, this is readily available from several sources and many libraries.

Nevertheless, the publishers believe the much more readable form into which Mr. Huntington's very words have been adapted will appeal to a far wider audience, for whose comfort and consolation this carefully edited work has been published.

Price £2.35 *(postage extra)*
(Laminated Cover)
Printed, sewn and bound
by the John Metcalfe Publishing Trust
ISBN 1 870039 24 6

SAVING FAITH

The sevenfold work of the Holy Ghost in bringing a sinner to saving faith in Christ opened and enlarged.

True faith is the work of God. False faith is the presumption of man. But where is the difference? *Saving Faith* shows the difference.

Price £2.25 *(postage extra)*
Paperback 250 pages
(Laminated Cover)
Printed, sewn and bound
by the John Metcalfe Publishing Trust
ISBN 1 870039 40 8

DELIVERANCE FROM THE LAW
THE WESTMINSTER CONFESSION EXPLODED

Deliverance from the law. A devastating vindication of the gospel of Christ against the traditions of man.

Price £1.90 *(postage extra)*
Paperback 160 pages
(Laminated Cover)
Printed, sewn and bound
by the John Metcalfe Publishing Trust
ISBN 1 870039 41 6

THE BEATITUDES

A unique insight destined to be the classic opening of this wonderful sequence of utterances from the lips of Jesus.

The reader will discover a penetration of the spiritual heights and divine depths of these peerless words in a way ever fresh and always rewarding though read time and time again.

Price £1.90 *(postage extra)*
Paperback 185 pages
(Laminated cover)
Printed, sewn and bound
by the John Metcalfe Publishing Trust
ISBN 1 870039 45 9

NEWLY PUBLISHED

PHILIPPIANS

The Epistle of Paul the Apostle to the Philippians is opened by this work from the pen of John Metcalfe with that lucid thoroughness which one has come to expect from a ministry received 'not of men, neither by man, but by the revelation of Jesus Christ'.

The work of God at Philippi is traced 'from the first day' until the time at which the epistle was written. Never were Lydia or the Philippian jailor drawn with more lively insight. The epistle itself is revealed in order, with passages—such as 'the mind that was in Christ Jesus'—that evidence the work of no less than a divine for our own times.

The Trustees give glory and thanks to God for the privilege of producing and subsidising this book.

Price £1.90 *(postage extra)*
Paperback 185 pages
(Laminated cover)
Printed, sewn and bound
by the John Metcalfe Publishing Trust
ISBN 1 870039 56 4

'TRACT FOR THE TIMES' SERIES

THE GOSPEL OF GOD

'TRACT FOR THE TIMES' SERIES

The Gospel of God. Beautifully designed, this tract positively describes the gospel under the following headings: The Gospel is of God; The Gospel is Entirely of God; The Gospel is Entire in Itself; The Gospel is Preached; The Gospel Imparts Christ; and, Nothing But the Gospel Imparts Christ.

Price 25p *(postage extra)*
(Laminated Cover)
No. 1 in the Series

THE STRAIT GATE

'TRACT FOR THE TIMES' SERIES

The Strait Gate. Exceptionally well made, this booklet consists of extracts from 'The Messiah', compiled in such a way as to challenge the shallowness of much of today's 'easy-believism', whilst positively pointing to the strait gate.

Price 25p *(postage extra)*
(Laminated Cover)
No. 2 in the Series

ETERNAL SONSHIP AND TAYLOR BRETHREN

'TRACT FOR THE TIMES' SERIES

Eternal Sonship and Taylor Brethren. This booklet is highly recommended, particularly for those perplexed by James Taylor's teaching against the eternal sonship of Christ.

Price 25p *(postage extra)*
(Laminated Cover)
No. 3 in the Series

MARKS OF THE NEW TESTAMENT CHURCH

'TRACT FOR THE TIMES' SERIES

Marks of the New Testament Church. This exposition from Acts 2:42 declares what were, and what were not, the abiding marks of the church. The apostles' doctrine, fellowship and ordinances are lucidly explained.

Price 25p *(postage extra)*
(Laminated Cover)
No. 4 in the Series

THE CHARISMATIC DELUSION

'TRACT FOR THE TIMES' SERIES

The Charismatic Delusion. A prophetic message revealing the fundamental error of this movement which has swept away so many in the tide of its popularity. Here the delusion is dispelled.

Price 25p *(postage extra)*
(Laminated Cover)
No. 5 in the Series

PREMILLENNIALISM EXPOSED

'TRACT FOR THE TIMES' SERIES

Premillennialism Exposed. Well received evangelically, particularly through the influence of J.N. Darby, the Schofield bible, and the Plymouth Brethren, Premillennialism has assumed the cloak of orthodoxy. In this tract the cloak is removed, and the unorthodoxy of this system is exposed. A remarkable revelation.

Price 25p *(postage extra)*
(Laminated Cover)
No. 6 in the Series

JUSTIFICATION AND PEACE

'TRACT FOR THE TIMES' SERIES

Justification and Peace. This tract is taken from a message preached in December 1984 at Penang Hill, Malaysia. In this well-known address, peace with God is seen to be based upon nothing save justification by faith. No one should miss this tract.

Price 25p *(postage extra)*
(Laminated Cover)
No. 7 in the Series

FAITH OR PRESUMPTION?

'TRACT FOR THE TIMES' SERIES

Faith or presumption? The eighth tract in this vital series exposes the difference between faith and presumption, showing that faith is not of the law, neither is is apart from the work of God, nor is it of man. The work of God in man that precedes saving faith is opened generally and particularly, and the tract goes on to reveal positively the nature of saving faith. Belief and 'easy-believism' are contrasted, making clear the difference between the two, as the system of presumption—called easy-believism—is clearly shown, and the way of true belief pointed out with lucid clarity.

Price 25p *(postage extra)*
(Laminated Cover)
No. 8 in the Series

THE ELECT UNDECEIVED

'TRACT FOR THE TIMES' SERIES

The Elect undeceived, the ninth Tract for the Times, earnestly contends for 'the faith once delivered to the saints' in a way that is spiritually edifying, positive, and subject to the Lord Jesus Christ according to the scriptures.

The Tract is a response to the pamphlet 'Salvation and the Church' published jointly by the Catholic Truth Society and Church House Publishing, in which the Anglican and Roman Catholic Commissioners agree together about JUSTIFICATION. The pamphlet shows how they have agreed.

Price 25p *(postage extra)*
(Laminated Cover)
No. 9 in the Series

JUSTIFYING RIGHTEOUSNESS

'TRACT FOR THE TIMES' SERIES

Justifying Righteousness. Was it wrought by the law of Moses or by the blood of Christ? Written not in the language of dead theology but that of the living God, here is the vital and experimental doctrine of the new testament. Part of the book 'Justification by Faith', nevertheless this tract has a message in itself essential to those who would know and understand the truth.

Price 25p *(postage extra)*
(Laminated Cover)
No. 10 in the Series

RIGHTEOUSNESS IMPUTED

'TRACT FOR THE TIMES' SERIES

Righteousness Imputed. The truth of the gospel and the fallacy of tradition. Here the gospel trumpet of the jubilee is sounded in no uncertain terms, as on the one hand that truth essential to be believed for salvation is opened from holy scripture, and on the other the errors of Brethrenism are brought to light in a unique and enlightening way. This tract is taken from the book 'Justification by Faith', but in itself it conveys a message of great penetration and clarity.

Price 25p *(postage extra)*
(Laminated Cover)
No. 11 in the Series

THE GREAT DECEPTION

'TRACT FOR THE TIMES' SERIES

The Great Deception. The erosion of Justification by faith. All ministers, every Christian, and each assembly ought not only to possess but to read and reread this prophetic message as the word of the Lord to this generation, set in the context of the age. This tract is part of the book 'Justification by Faith' but contains within itself a message which is at once vital and authoritative.

Price 25p *(postage extra)*
(Laminated Cover)
No. 12 in the Series

A FAMINE IN THE LAND

'TRACT FOR THE TIMES' SERIES

A Famine in the Land. Taken from the Book of Ruth, with telling forcefulness this tract opens conditions exactly parallel to those of our own times. 'Behold, the days come, saith the Lord GOD, that I will send a famine in the land, not a famine of bread, nor a thirst for water, but of hearing the words of the LORD: and they shall wander from sea to sea, and from the north even to the east, they shall run to and fro to seek the word of the LORD, and shall not find it.'

Price 25p *(postage extra)*
(Laminated Cover)
No. 13 in the Series

BLOOD AND WATER

'TRACT FOR THE TIMES' SERIES

Blood and Water. Of the four gospels, only John reveals the truth that blood was shed at the cross. When it was shed, Jesus was dead already. With the blood there came forth water. But what do these things mean? With devastating present-day application, this tract tells you what they mean.

Price 25p *(postage extra)*
(Laminated Cover)
No. 14 in the Series

WOMEN BISHOPS?

'TRACT FOR THE TIMES' SERIES

Women Bishops? This is a question that has arisen in America, but should it have arisen at all?
Read this tract and find out the authoritative answer.

Price 25p *(postage extra)*
(Laminated Cover)
No. 15 in the Series

THE HEAVENLY VISION

'TRACT FOR THE TIMES' SERIES

The Heavenly Vision not only transformed the prophet himself, it became a savour of life unto life—or death unto death—to all the people.
'*Where there is no vision the people perish*', Proverbs 29:18. This is true. But where is the vision today? And what is the vision today? This tract answers those questions.

Price 25p *(Postage extra)*
(Laminated Cover)
No. 16 in the Series

EVANGELICAL TRACTS

EVANGELICAL TRACTS

1. **The Two Prayers of Elijah.** Green card cover, price 10p.

2. **Wounded for our Transgressions.** Gold card cover, price 10p.

3. **The Blood of Sprinkling.** Red card cover, price 10p.

4. **The Grace of God that brings Salvation.** Blue card cover, price 10p.

5. **The Name of Jesus.** Rose card cover, price 10p.

6. **The Ministry of the New Testament.** Purple card cover, price 10p.

7. **The Death of the Righteous** (*The closing days of J.B. Stoney*) by A.M.S. (his daughter). Ivory card cover, Price 10p.

8. **Repentance.** Sky blue card cover, price 10p.

9. **Legal Deceivers Exposed.** Crimson card cover, price 10p.

10. **Unconditional Salvation.** Green card cover, price 10p.

11. **Religious Merchandise.** Brown card cover, price 10p.

12. **Comfort.** Pink card cover, price 10p.

13. **Peace.** Grey card cover, price 10p.

14. **Eternal Life.** Cobalt card cover, price 10p.

15. **The Handwriting of Ordinances.** Fawn card cover, price 10p.

16. **'Lord, Lord!'.** Emerald card cover, price 10p.

ECCLESIA TRACTS

ECCLESIA TRACTS

The Beginning of the Ecclesia by John Metcalfe. No. 1 in the Series, Sand grain cover, Price 10p.

Churches and the Church by J.N. Darby. Edited. No. 2 in the Series, Sand grain cover, Price 10p.

The Ministers of Christ by John Metcalfe. No. 3 in the Series, Sand grain cover, Price 10p.

The Inward Witness by George Fox. Edited. No. 4 in the Series, Sand grain cover, Price 10p.

The Notion of a Clergyman by J.N. Darby. Edited. No. 5 in the Series, Sand grain cover, Price 10p.

The Servant of the Lord by William Huntington. Edited and Abridged. No. 6 in the Series, Sand grain cover, Price 10p.

One Spirit by William Kelly. Edited. No. 7 in the Series, Sand grain cover, Price 10p.

The Funeral of Arminianism by William Huntington. Edited and Abridged. No. 8 in the Series, Sand grain cover, Price 10p.

One Body by William Kelly. Edited. No. 9 in the Series, Sand grain cover, Price 10p.

False Churches and True by John Metcalfe. No. 10 in the Series, Sand grain cover, Price 10p.

Separation from Evil by J.N. Darby. Edited. No. 11 in the Series, Sand grain cover, Price 10p.

The Remnant by J.B. Stoney. Edited. No. 12 in the Series, Sand grain cover, Price 10p.

The Arminian Skeleton by William Huntington. Edited and Abridged. No. 13 in the Series, Sand grain cover, Price 10p.

FOUNDATION TRACTS

FOUNDATION TRACTS

1. **Female Priests?** by John Metcalfe. Oatmeal cover, price 25p.

2. **The Bondage of the Will** by Martin Luther. Translated and Abridged. Oatmeal cover, price 25p.

3. **Of the Popish Mass** by John Calvin. Translated and Abridged. Oatmeal cover, price 25p.

4. **The Adversary** by John Metcalfe. Oatmeal cover, price 25p.

MINISTRY BY JOHN METCALFE

TAPE MINISTRY BY JOHN METCALFE
FROM ENGLAND AND THE FAR EAST
IS AVAILABLE.

In order to obtain this free recorded ministry, please send your blank cassette (C.90) and the cost of the return postage, including your name and address in block capitals, to the John Metcalfe Publishing Trust, Church Road, Tylers Green, Penn, Bucks, HP10 8LN. Tapelists are available on request.

Owing to the increased demand for the tape ministry, we are unable to supply more than two tapes per order, except in the case of meetings for the hearing of tapes, where a special arrangement can be made.

THE MINISTRY OF THE NEW TESTAMENT

The purpose of this substantial A4 gloss paper magazine is to provide spiritual and experimental ministry with sound doctrine which rightly and prophetically divides the Word of Truth.

Readers of our books will already know the high standards of our publications. They can be confident that these pages will maintain that quality, by giving access to enduring ministry from the past, much of which is derived from sources that are virtually unobtainable today, and publishing a living ministry from the present. Selected articles from the following writers have already been included:

Eli Ashdown · Abraham Booth · John Bradford
John Bunyan · John Burgon · John Calvin · Donald Cargill
John Cennick · J.N. Darby · George Fox · John Foxe
William Gadsby · John Guthrie · William Guthrie
Grey Hazlerigg · William Huntington · William Kelly
John Kennedy · John Kershaw · Hanserd Knollys · James Lewis
Martin Luther · Robert Murray McCheyne · John Metcalfe
Alexander—Sandy—Peden · J.C. Philpot · J.K. Popham
James Renwick · J.B. Stoney · Henry Tanner
Arthur Triggs · John Vinall · John Warburton
John Welwood · George Whitefield · J.A. Wylie

Price £1.75 *(postage included)*
Issued Spring, Summer, Autumn, Winter.

Book Order Form

Please send to the address below:-

		Price	Quantity
A Question for Pope John Paul II		£1.25	......
Of God or Man?		£1.45	......
Noah and the Flood		£1.90	......
Divine Footsteps		£0.95	......
The Red Heifer		£0.75	......
The Wells of Salvation		£1.50	......
The Book of Ruth (Hardback edition)		£4.95	......
Divine Meditations of William Huntington		£2.35	......
Present-Day Conversions of the New Testament Kind		£2.25	......
Saving Faith		£2.25	......
Deliverance from the Law		£1.90	......
The Beatitudes		£1.90	......
Colossians		£0.95	......
Philippians		£1.90	......
Matthew		£0.95	......
Psalms, Hymns & Spiritual Songs (Hardback edition)			
The Psalms of the Old Testament		£2.50	......
Spiritual Songs from the Gospels		£2.50	......
The Hymns of the New Testament		£2.50	......
'Apostolic Foundation of the Christian Church' series			
Foundations Uncovered	Vol.I	£0.75	......
The Birth of Jesus Christ	Vol.II	£0.95	......
The Messiah (Hardback edition)	Vol.III	£7.75	......
The Son of God and Seed of David (Hardback edition)	Vol.IV	£6.95	......
Christ Crucified (Hardback edition)	Vol.V	£6.95	......
Justification by Faith (Hardback edition)	Vol.VI	£7.50	......
The Church: What is it? (Hardback edition)	Vol.VII	£7.75	......

Name and Address (in block capitals)

....

....

....

If money is sent with order please allow for postage. Please address to:- The John Metcalfe Publishing Trust, Church Road, Tylers Green, Penn, Bucks, HP10 8LN.

Tract Order Form

Please send to the address below:-

Evangelical Tracts		Price	Quantity
The Two Prayers of Elijah		£0.10	......
Wounded for our Transgressions		£0.10	......
The Blood of Sprinkling		£0.10	......
The Grace of God that Brings Salvation		£0.10	......
The Name of Jesus		£0.10	......
The Ministry of the New Testament		£0.10	......
The Death of the Righteous by A.M.S.		£0.10	......
Repentance		£0.10	......
Legal Deceivers Exposed		£0.10	......
Unconditional Salvation		£0.10	......
Religious Merchandise		£0.10	......
Comfort		£0.10	......
Peace		£0.10	......
Eternal Life		£0.10	......
The Handwriting of Ordinances		£0.10	......
'Lord, Lord!'		£0.10	......
'Tract for the Times' series			
The Gospel of God	No.1	£0.25	......
The Strait Gate	No.2	£0.25	......
Eternal Sonship and Taylor Brethren	No.3	£0.25	......
Marks of the New Testament Church	No.4	£0.25	......
The Charismatic Delusion	No.5	£0.25	......
Premillennialism Exposed	No.6	£0.25	......
Justification and Peace	No.7	£0.25	......
Faith or presumption?	No.8	£0.25	......
The Elect undeceived	No.9	£0.25	......
Justifying Righteousness	No.10	£0.25	......
Righteousness Imputed	No.11	£0.25	......
The Great Deception	No.12	£0.25	......
A Famine in the Land	No.13	£0.25	......
Blood and Water	No.14	£0.25	......
Women Bishops?	No.15	£0.25	......
The Heavenly Vision	No.16	£0.25	......

Name and Address (in block capitals)

....

....

....

If money is sent with order please allow for postage. Please address to:- The John Metcalfe Publishing Trust, Church Road, Tylers Green, Penn, Bucks, HP10 8LN.

cut here

Tract Order Form

Please send to the address below:-

		Price	Quantity
Ecclesia Tracts			
The Beginning of the Ecclesia	No.1	£0.10	......
Churches and the Church (J.N.D.)	No.2	£0.10	......
The Ministers of Christ	No.3	£0.10	......
The Inward Witness (G.F.)	No.4	£0.10	......
The Notion of a Clergyman (J.N.D.)	No.5	£0.10	......
The Servant of the Lord (W.H.)	No.6	£0.10	......
One Spirit (W.K.)	No.7	£0.10	......
The Funeral of Arminianism (W.H.)	No.8	£0.10	......
One Body (W.K.)	No.9	£0.10	......
False Churches and True	No.10	£0.10	......
Separation from Evil (J.N.D.)	No.11	£0.10	......
The Remnant (J.B.S.)	No.12	£0.10	......
The Arminian Skeleton (W.H.)	No.13	£0.10	......
Foundation Tracts			
Female Priests?	No.1	£0.25	......
The Bondage of the Will (Martin Luther)	No.2	£0.25	......
Of the Popish Mass (John Calvin)	No.3	£0.25	......
The Adversary	No.4	£0.25	......

Name and Address (in block capitals)

. . . .

. . . .

. . . .

If money is sent with order please allow for postage. Please address to:- The John Metcalfe Publishing Trust, Church Road, Tylers Green, Penn, Bucks, HP10 8LN.

cut here

Magazine Order Form

Name and Address (in block capitals)

....

....

....

Please send me .... current copy/copies of The Ministry of the New Testament.

Please send me .... year/s subscription.

I enclose a cheque/postal order for £ ....

(Price: including postage, U.K. £1.75; Overseas £1.90)
(One year's subscription: Including postage, U.K. £7.00; Overseas £7.60)

Cheques should be made payable to The John Metcalfe Publishing Trust, and for overseas subscribers should be in pounds sterling drawn on a London Bank.

10 or more copies to one address will qualify for a 10% discount

Back numbers from Spring 1986 available.

Please send to The John Metcalfe Publishing Trust, Church Road, Tylers Green, Penn, Bucks, HP10 8LN

All Publications of the Trust are subsidised by the Publishers.